GENERATIONS

Generations
The Time Machine in Theory and Practice

JUDITH BURNETT
University of Wolverhampton, UK

ASHGATE

Published by
Ashgate Publishing Limited
Wey Court East
Union Road
Farnham
Surrey, GU9 7PT
England

Ashgate Publishing Company
Suite 420
101 Cherry Street
Burlington
VT 05401-4405
USA

www.ashgate.com

British Library Cataloguing in Publication Data
Burnett, Judith.
  Generations : the time machine in theory and practice.
  1. Generations. 2. Social structure. 3. Social change.
  I. Title
  305.2-dc22

Library of Congress Cataloging-in-Publication Data
Burnett, Judith.
  Generations : the time machine in theory and practice / by Judith Burnett.
    p. cm.
  Includes index.
  ISBN 978-0-7546-7456-6 (hbk.) -- ISBN 978-1-4094-0980-9
  (ebook) 1. Generations. 2. Time--Sociological aspects. I. Title.

  HM721.B87 2010
  305.2--dc22

2010009587

ISBN 9780754674566 (hbk)
ISBN 9781409409809 (ebk)

Mixed Sources
Product group from well-managed
forests and other controlled sources
www.fsc.org Cert no. SGS-COC-2482
© 1996 Forest Stewardship Council
FSC

Printed and bound in Great Britain by
TJ International Ltd, Padstow, Cornwall

Contents

List of Figures

List of Tables

List of Abbreviations

ACORN	A Classification Of Residential Neighbourhoods
BEF	The British Expeditionary Force
BSRA	British Society for Research on Ageing
CCCS	Centre for Contemporary Cultural Studies
EE	Emotional Energy
GLBT	Gay Lesbian Bi-Sexual and Transgendered
IAG	International Association of Gerontology
MCS	The Millennium Cohort Study
NCDS	National Child Development Study
NSHD	Survey of Health and Development
WFA	Western Front Association

Introduction

Once the *Introduction* to a book such as this might start with the definition of a term, a brief etymology, and an anchor in a body of theory. But where a book which explores the concept of generation should begin is a different matter. All books are written through the lenses of the times in which they are produced. It would be a sorry book on generations which set this to one side and thus overlooked the implicit standpoints of author and reader as the insiders and outsiders of our own generational location and the collective authors of our unique generational experiences. Such standpoints might influence how we approach a book such as this, with our prior knowledge, assumptions and expectations including what we might think the book is 'about'.

Googling the word 'generation' can tell us of the uses of the word in popular circulation right now (albeit weighted for internet users as a section of the population): Googling *Generation* produces - Y; - Gap; - Star Trek movie; - estate agents; - myths; - Reform; and - family tree. Changing the term slightly produces lots more delicious leads: Googling *Generations* produces - South Africa; - soap; and - of i-pod. *Generational* produces - Dynamics; - Theory; - Biblical Curses; - Conflict; - Differences; and - My. Googling *Generation Of* produces - 1898; - Chaos; - electricity; - 1960s; and - companies.

The concept of generation, like all language, is mutable. For social scientists generation is a dual concept, referring to both family and kinship structures on the one hand, and cohorts (or age sets) on the other. It has been subject to change in the flow of history and circumstance in which it has been put to work. The concept of generation has been charged with being too empty and slippery to be of much use; yet these characteristics are a function of its survival over thousands of years and the diversity of human formation and experience which it has named.

For such a potentially unstable concept, generation also displays a surprising degree of continuity. At its heart lies a concept of self and time which captures something of the essence of the human condition. Firstly, we think of ourselves as individual and yet co-exist in a collective universe we conceptualise as society. Thus, we are both an 'I' and a 'We', simultaneously. Secondly, we develop corporeal awareness in infancy and finitude in childhood. In other words, we know that we are born, we live, and we die. This is the case even though the social stream is apparently unending as society flows with a continual replacement largely invisible to the naked eye at a macro and collective level. Thirdly, our co-existence is lived out in the company of a time based cohort of contemporaries in a two-legged race consisting of both a kinship network which structures us in time on a diachronic axis and an age set network which structures us in time on a synchronic axis, see Figure I.1 below.

In the figure below we see structure A–B articulating lineage by descent through generations of offspring. This is a diachronic relationship where time is assumed to be moving from A to B. In this model our immediate family is clustered at various points around X while our ancestors (in the western conception of 'back in time') are clustered around A and its environs. Axis C–D represents the other meaning of generation, as a cohort. This is a synchronic relationship which under the conditions of modernity became expressed as a historical generation. In this figure, each of us as individuals is located at point X, having a position in both the kinship system and the cohort system, simultaneously. Our identification and belonging to this constellation may wax and wane over the lifetime: indeed, one of the spurs to writing this book was the recognition that we know remarkably little about how this happens, why, or with what consequences. In these ways we are organised in and out by complex systems of structure and agency; obligation and exchange; reciprocity and the exercise of power.

The social potential of such a system is largely unknowable but is a rich vein of exploration for even the most casual visitor. After all, lateral systems of time based cohorts can and have obtained velocity and identity, becoming a social force in their own right. Vertical systems of kinship allow the reproduction of inheritance and systems of stratification as well as the physical and identity reproduction of the tribe, while both systems provide for intimacy and conflict; the markers of boundaries; and the constant re-creation of the We, the I, the Them and the Us.

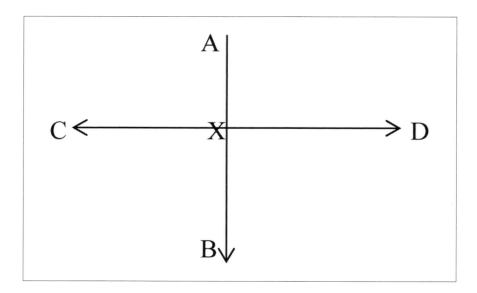

Figure I.1 Conceptual systems of generations

Both meanings of the concept of generation (familial and cohort based) catch at the temporal structure of social life. This book explores these qualities of generations primarily through the window of sociology and its cognate disciplines, and provides a slim survey of a few examples of both the concept of generation and the actuality of generations through the process of entering and exiting society.

The Sociological Concept of Generation

The concept of generation belongs to the cluster of lifecourse, cohort and generation, which attempt to address the temporal and historically specific qualities of social life. Conceptual distinction can be problematic. Cohorts are typically constructed by external systems such as research, the military, and the education system (see Ryder 1965), generations are unique entities which for Mannheim [1927] (1952) become actualised. Cohorts are imagined by researchers and made by systems, generations are constituted by actors who become aware of their history. A further complication is the dual meaning of generation: an age set meaning and a familial meaning which became separated and specialised through the development of social theory and sociology.

Modern generation analysis was claimed by Mannheim (1952) as a problem for sociology. His was a characterisation as a cohort based approach and has a particular interest in the subjective consciousness of the actors and their ability to act upon the social understandings which they have developed. Mannheim states that generation is a social location that has the potential to affect an individual's consciousness in much the same way as social class. He describes an intersection between biology and society (Pilcher 1994) in that 'individuals who belong to the same generation, who share the same year of birth, are endowed, to that extent, with a common location in the historical dimension of the social process' (Mannheim 1927/1952:105). It is this common location which presents common social problems to the generation, requiring of them creative solutions and adaptive strategies (Elder 1974) in order to get by. This process leads to the generation's recognition of its own positionality and thus allows it to develop strategic responses, to become actualised as a strategic generation (Edmunds and Turner 2002b).

However, the whole of this cluster of concepts share a major concern with the intersection of biography and history, famously identified by Mills (1959) as a foundational concern of the sociological imagination. Indeed, it is precisely this ability to span macro and micro levels of analysis that makes working with the concept of generation potentially rewarding, and leads Pilcher (1995:481) to regard Mannheim's work as an undervalued legacy observing that '... scant attention has been paid to the sociology of generations by British sociologists'. This intersection also allows us to reflect upon the dual character of the generation concept and to recognise that while Mannheim's formulation was largely concerned with the Axis C–D, in fact much post-war study of generation also explores the intersection of C–D activity with axis A–B. Shifts in one cause shifts in another, and the generational system as a system is seen as a complex one characterised by reiterative processes.

Guide to the Book

The book begins with an invitation to 'meet the ancestors' in the contexts of ancient and pre-modern concepts of time and space. In this we see that the concept of generations is an old one, dating back a few thousand years. While there is something of the sense of a cohort about it, it does not reflect our modern idea of a cohort based generation as occupying a narrow slice of time. Rather, the concept refers to certain kinds of people who lived in a certain period, whose attributes could be 'read' rather like one might read the weather or the stars. This establishes the concept as associated with time periods, but the concept of time periods itself is rooted even earlier. The mythic structure of beliefs in Ancient Egyptian culture provided for a continuous time, largely split between a brief present and an eternal afterlife. Accessing the afterlife was a critical matter by which a life force or entity might continue to 'exist'. A substantive human past, and the notion that citizens may contribute (however partially) towards the present came later, and with it a changing orientation to change.

The chapter moves onto consider the emergence of a lineage concept of generation and its interweaving into the imagery of Christianity with the Tree of Jesse, which establishes both the concept of the one true line of descent (and a system for sidelining competitive siblings) and the family tree. This meshes with concepts of personhood and the idea that persons may have lives of their 'own'.

Chapter 2 turns to consider how the concept of generation was treated in the rise of social science and early sociology, and the intellectual and social changes in the concept of time and space which led to the formation of a nineteenth century concept of generation. It is noted that time itself dramatically expanded with the 'discoveries' of geological time and Darwin's theory of evolution, while on the other hand becoming subject to unification and synchronisation as a result of the processes of industrialisation: clock time, timetables, transport and the establishment of industrial time. However, synchronisation also threw up significant difficulties, for example clashes between rural time and industrial time, leading ultimately to a splitting and segmentation of time. Personhood and the organisation of a life, a week and a day were thus subject to both unification and splitting.

The generation concept survived this with aplomb, boosted by Darwin's imagery of the tree-like structure of descent and the appearance of the first youthful circles, gangs and groups in urban centres.

Mannheim's intervention lifted the concept of generation out of biology and folklore and transported it into sociology, presenting as it does a sociological problem of the reiterative relationships between structure and agency. Mannheim's view was a cohort based one, and in keeping with his moment in modernity he largely historicised the concept.

Following the Second World War we can see further developments in the career of the concept of generation. Chapter 3 explores the post-war specialisation of sociology and its cognate disciplines in its lines of enquiry through the family of temporal concepts to create sub-fields focused on different levels of analysis and styles. These lines are persons with lifecycles (later termed lifecourses); the cohort; and the generation.

After exploring the differences and overlaps between them, Chapter 3 explores the three major approaches to generation studies. The first of these, *Generations as Social Agency*, captures an action orientated approach, casting generations as gaining velocity and impacting the system in its search for new scripts and different meanings. I suggest that the 1960s Boomer generation influenced the thinking about generations in this direction, producing much of the implicit assumptions about the wave like nature of generations and their propensity to intergenerational conflict and radicalism.

The second approach, however, shows diversity in generational life. *Generations as Inter-Generational Structure* show activity of both a cohort and familial kind, drawing together the two to understand generational systems as integrated systems of reciprocity and exchange in the context of stratification and possible conflict over resources on the one hand, and identification, affective relationships and belonging on the other. This trope has been boosted by critical social gerontology and new kinds of studies of generations which are less focused on youth as such, and invite us to reflect upon what the future of generations may hold.

The third approach, *Generational Map-Making*, refers to representations of society through a generational structure, where a series of abutting generations make their way through regimes of changeable kinds. These maps do not allow for the reality of messy and porous boundaries of generations in practice, but do allow us to see constellations of generations at work over long periods of time in a potentially interesting manner.

The focus of Chapter 4 is the generation of the Great War of 1914–18, one of the highly constructed and remembered generations, such that Wohl's concept of it being in effect a magnetic field seems relevant. I argue that this generation is an exemplar of the inter-war manifestations of generations: Epic Generations. At once modern and tragic, these generations are cast as history makers, caught up in their moment and with social tasks to perform which stand in contrast to the Consumption Generations which were to follow the Second World War.

The implication for the generation concept was important, since the Great War in effect democratised the concept which came to refer to the working class multitudes as well as the elites of the upper class families. Secondly, the generation concept also became secularised, leaving behind the feudalism of Christianity and the religious quality of the family tree. The chapter explores how the generation concept was built, looking at the social processes of memory and mind; the cult of literature; bodies and sites of memory; and the museumification of the generation of the Western Front – in contrast to that of the Isonzo front in the Soca Valley, Slovenia.

In Chapters 5 and 6 I turn my attention to what I have come to see as the Consumption Generations of post-war society. Built through the market and neither tragic nor historical in quite the way of the earlier twentieth century the Boomers operate in ways which are 'the same but different'. I identify two segments of the Boomers, a first wave (Chapter 5) and a second wave (Chapter 6). These two waves were the outcome of the change in the social situation which each encountered at the youthful moment, the first in boom the second in bust. I note the more ephemeral quality of the Boomers in form and deed, although the first wave secures names and social space more readily than the second, and finds more historical projects with which to engage. The second wave are particularly ephemeral, and their activity begins to open up questions about the nature of generation theory in sociology which has traditionally looked to the youthful moment as the moment of generational identification, expression, and consequence.

Chapter 7 turns finally to the implications for the generation concept of a potentially spectacular and possibly underrated fact that we now live in the contexts of ageing societies. While this is occurring at different rates and speeds and its stratification is both critically important and a matter of social justice, nonetheless it is to be noted that this appears to be a global trend.

This raises a number of highly interesting problems for the generation concept, whether for action theories; inter-generational structures which have been built on certain concepts of taxation and institutionalised care; or map making concepts which track regime change driven by the state (first half of twentieth century); market (second half of twentieth century); and civil society, at the level of household and community (although its intimations are there in feminism and its movements). I note that much of generation work has been about youth and often male youth at that. Yet the future seems to lie with the elders, and a female constituency at that. This suggests that we may yet need to revisit the concept and be ready to rewrite the history books of the future to accommodate yet new forms of generationalism, sights as yet unseen, form as yet unknowable.

In the Conclusions I briefly indicate some further lines of inquiry thrown up by the book but not explored here. These include the problem of Silent Generations and Interim or Buffer Generations. Turning first to Silent Generations, these are potential age set or kinship groups which for whatever reason don't mobilise, and thus do not become actualised in Mannheim's sense, or empowered and visible in a more general sense. One of the difficulties with this is the possible explanations lying with how we see generations or more truly how we recognise them. The existence of Silent Generations might be explicable by the idea of authenticity and thus the authentic generation. These will behave in appropriately 'generationish' way i.e. can achieve recognition within existing scripts which pull on registers of meaning which indicate generationalism. Thus, one possibility is that in practice few generations are silent in a sociological sense. This raises questions about what filters are at work in recognition and possibly the standpoint of the holders of filters. However, an equally plausible explanation may lie with the failure of actualisation as a sociological event. This line of thought would suggest that while generations may have the potential to become realised some do not. The range of variables and circumstances which provide them to do so or not do so would then form the basis of a study. However in researching this book I have found very few examples of studies of silent generations *per se*. By and large the research problem is formulated around generations which make an appearance. Perhaps I am suggesting here that they make an appearance – in our line of vision. This is an age old problem in research in the social sciences from which the generation field is not excluded.

Secondly, turning to Interim or Buffer Generations, I refer to the occasional sighting of generations which fall between 'major' others. These 'bookends' can bring change and thus an ending to the previous generation, as well as providing a range of bridging mechanisms to provide for its continuity. On the other hand, interim generations may share some characteristics with silent generations: how would we distinguish between these categories of actors? The sociological function as an interim network may be to provide an interval or beat, which then allows the next generation to coalesce, hence the sense of social bookends. These ideas however run counter to most orthodox generation theory: far from an action model or a structural, age set model their function and historical task appears to lie with fulfilling and maintaining, but within parameters. But how are those parameters maintained, and how can we understand the role of coeval generations which lie silent? Sociology, with its concept of the social thought through frameworks of macro–micro and agency and structure may struggle to accommodate that silence.

The book aims to show how the study of the generation in concept and in practice deepens our understandings of lived experience as conducted through communities of time which bind us together in a two legged race on the one hand, and split and segment us on the other. The generation concept represents a way to think about dwelling in its aspect of living in, and through, time and space. For sociology, the generation concept is meshed with both our awareness of ourselves as a mammalian species of humanity with concepts such as mortal bodies and consciousness which has a capacity to be both an I and a We. This stratified consciousness stands in relation to our puzzle that we, the body, live and die while we, the universe, is in continual flight which predates and outlives 'us'. These concepts allow us to challenge sociology in its preference and origins of theorising based on an homogenous present to re-imagining the social as dynamic and multiversal.

In conclusion I can say that this book has begun to map out how generational formations manifest differently in relation to the changing social system. Thus we see a mutability to the concept of generation itself, partly because it is contested and partly because what it tries to talk about keeps changing. I have identified the possibility of different genres or kinds of generations, in particular Epic Generations, and Consumption Generations. I have observed our lack of secure understandings as to how and why and under what circumstances velocity and actualisation may or may not be achieved and am horribly aware that much of this book in practice looks at the experiences of European and US formations and rather cursorily at that. This is a matter of regret although is explicable as a problem of bandwidth and scale in the contexts of a substantial and unfinished project as things currently stand. This exploration has shown me the richness of the vein of inquiry which the generation concept affords. Yet of all that I have learned, there is one fact which is incontrovertible: a book such as this raises more questions than it answers.

Chapter 1
Meet the Ancestors:
Real and Imagined

The concept of generations is an old one which historically sought to address the fact of human existence which occurs in slices of time. It is a concept to which time and space relationships are integral. It speaks of human self understandings as experiencing life as collective and individual in the contexts of co-existence and relatedness.

This chapter explores the categorisation of the universe which allowed the concept first of time and then of *human* time to emerge alongside the concept of qualities or attributes which could be given to time. It considers perspectives on time and the universe in Ancient Greece and Egypt, and how generations may have been regarded as entities which could be 'read', rather like the gods, the wind and the moon. Ancestor worship was common in ancient cultures and we can also locate the concept of generations in this context. The chapter next turns to consider the rise of the concept of lineage, which is gradually represented visually in images of the tree. The tree-like paradigm was popularised in the West by Christianity and was passed down to underpin descriptions of the systems of relatedness such as family and kinship. Individuals with identities defined by their location in the kinship network emerged, in due course with personalities. The seasons of life were complemented by the masks of life, and the lifecourse which individuals 'have' or 'do', and generations or cohorts into which 'we' are embedded.

Pre-Modernity: The Use of the Concept of Generations

Nash (1978) argues that the origins of the concept of generation stems from Ancient Greece, although I suggest it can be further traced back to Ancient Egypt. However, Nash takes, for example, references to generations in Homer's *Iliad*, where Glaucus responds to Diomedes' identity challenge by locating himself within his ancestry – the more general 'generations of men':

> Greathearted son of Tydeus, why do you question my lineage [*genea*]?
> As is the generation [*genea*] of leaves, so too of men:
> At one time the wind shakes the leaves to the ground,
> but then the flourishing woods
> Gives birth, and the season of spring comes into existence [*epigignetai*];

So it is of the generations of men, which alternately
come forth and pass away.

Homer, *Iliad*, book 6, lines 145–49, in Nash (1978:1)

Nash argues that ancient Greek, Latin and English usage of generation (*genos, genea, genesis, gone, genus, generatio*, etc.), carry a range of meanings including 'birth and reproduction to age, time of life, cycle of life, race, family, or even species' (ibid: 2). Nash also suggests that the 'words stem from a common Indo-European root' (**gen-, o-grade, *gone-, zero grade, *gn* Sanskit janab), the fundamental meaning of which is 'to come into existence' (ibid: 2). However, generation also marked identity borders, 'allegiance, time of life, span of years, sameness with one group and otherness from the rest' (ibid: 2). Instantly we see one of the defining characteristics of the concept of generation, its duality, where it refers to both family descent and age sets. It explains the arrival and departure of one cohort after another in the context of a continuous social stream. The concept of time is implicitly present. Firstly, since each cohort experiences finitude while the social stream flows for eternity. Secondly, since offspring are born in one period to a parental family which produces offspring of kin, but are continuously born in wider society, which produces offspring of kith.

A second feature of the concept is its timescapes. Timescapes, as discussed by Adam (1998), demonstrate the way in which consequences and social outgrowths lie latent, to be manifested years or epochs later. In particular, Adam discusses environmental disasters in this context. However, the concept lends itself to discussions of generations, a concept which does not readily fit into short term timeframes or social actions and dynamics which occur in a uniform manner according to tidy units of time. Take, for example, the repercussions of the adventures of one generation produces consequences further down the line in time for another. For example, defeat in battle may be avenged by a subsequent generation. Another case would be the socio economic and cultural transmission which occurs between generations. The starting point of one generation affects its ability to provide leverage to its offspring.

This positionality of generations is not consistently understood or synthesised in the literature on generations, yet is clearly recognised in folk tales and lay accounts which express inter-generational relationships and their consequences over time. In this sense, generations form a system of relationships which span time, their narratives and memory providing connecting threads in culture laid over actual structures and major organising systems. What we learn from this is the use of the concept of generations as a quasi-sociological account, presented as collective legends of the tribe as well as its possible function at the level of ideology, providing explanations for the state of affairs encountered in the present. These ancient stories of generations may tell us much about the dastardly and even heroic deeds of the time which caused what we would call social change to occur (for example a regime change, a change of ruler, or a change of land ownership and so on) but provided little basis for change in the present.

Ancient Greek and Ancient Egyptian Civilisation

These concepts of social groups with an identity and location in time prefigure the modern concept of the human universe. Ancient Greek beliefs accommodated human succession and had a concept of history made by people limited and informed by certain categories of other kinds of entities. Ancient Greek mythological accounts talk of generations among a range of creatures and spirits through which the history of its civilisation is told. Hesiod's account *Works and Days* (Hesiod and West 1999) gives an account of the ages of man. These start with the generations of the golden period (the offspring of Cronos, who were forever young) succeeded by the silver generations (the offspring of the Olympians) who followed first and bronze (a warlike people) subsequently. These three generations were followed by an interim generation characterised as heroic and then an iron generation.

The time of each generation was not as literally counted as in the modern sense. A 'generation' may have referred to a sequence of generations the sum total of which expressed something Secondly, generational activity is acknowledged as human however are tempered by awesome gods who essentially played with the pawns of men: thus we can say that history was not 'made' by 'the people' in the modern sense which the concept of generation acquired when it became historicised through modernity. However the concept of generations expresses and indicates both the passage of time and change, as well as providing boundary markers of what I suggest we can understand as being 'kinds of people' who lived in 'kinds of times'.

Alongside the concept of generations expressing time and change, we also see that early on they were described by attributes. Time and attributes were therefore entwined and can be seen in action in time pieces such as the Athenian horologion, the *Tower of the Four Winds*. The Tower contained a water clock, sun dial and weather vanes, and was used to read the universe as part of a system in which the passage of time was integrally linked to night, day, the weather, and the passage of the seasons.

This allows us to understand that ancient and pre-modern concept of generation may have been very different from ours. Generations were entities which could be 'read', as the weather or the stars could be 'read'. Similarly, we can see that they are endowed with properties (youthful, weak, heroic, fast etc.); they might have been regarded as portents of what is to come or blamed for events which occurred, the genaeology of which could be traced back to them. In this way, the pre-modern concept of generation seems to lack either accurate or significant accounting of time in the modern sense of units or periods, but rather phases which were somehow distinctive.

The generation concept was subsequently to develop its modern meanings: separated from the category of nature and the universe, generations were to become exclusively human and historical. The question of the time to be associated with generations became problematised much later. The time of Ancient Greek mythology may implicitly be hundreds or even thousands of years. Yet Mannheim encountered the timespan defined by the culture of the nineteenth century, and a debate as to whether it is twenty or thirty years (a debate he dismissed as not particularly relevant). In the late twentieth century, this moved again. For example, if the timespan is defined by procreation ('nature') then perhaps it is every twenty or thirty years. But if it is defined by consumption, discourse and other identity systems ('nurture') then perhaps the space which elapses between generations has shrunk to being as brief as every ten years, and it is possible to imagine generations as now a different kind of entity to even those of the industrial period, let alone earlier.

The mutability of the timespan coupled with the vagueness of the meaning of the concept of generation has been viewed in some quarters as one of the weaknesses of the concept of generation, further evidence of its instability and slipperyness. However, such preoccupation with time and the need to quantify the timespan of generations is itself to read the concept of generation through the cultural lens of the present with its own, specific meanings of the generation concept as a time-based concept defined by the concept of time which we have. In other words, this is a modern problem with the concept of generation. As such, it is largely invented by the moderns.

The Ancient Greek formulation was in part the result of a civilisation characterised by complexity and a relatively wide geographical reach, as well as one which inherited key ideas from the Ancient Egyptian civilisation regarding a spiritual universe.

The Ancient Egyptian state endured for at least three thousand years in its unified form and for another thousand previously as two or more states. The civilisation passed through distinctive periods of Kingdoms and dynasties. Nonetheless, the core of Egyptian belief and social organisation is notable for its continuity as much as change even though the fear of change (which was interpreted as disorder) was substantial (Kemp 2006).

In Ancient Egypt, developing shared concepts of time was important, since this allowed two things, firstly the organisation of agriculture and using the rise and fall of the Nile for which prediction was needed, and secondly, to facilitate religious rituals to occur. Religious rituals were the one of the major lubricating oils of Ancient Egypt. They provided for the passage of time to be constructed by creating 'before and after' periods of time as bookends to magical, transformative events as well as accounting for the passage of time through mythic narratives which provided explanations for the events of the universe and thus indications of how life should be lived including the holding of rituals. The timing of rituals was provided for by the use of objects (both flat dishes and pillars such as obelisks) as sundials; the astronomical instrument the merkhet which allowed the movement of stars to be tracked; and the innovation of the first water clocks which allowed for greater accuracy in timing the rituals particularly feasts in the hours of darkness. The Egyptian calendar may have been based upon the cycle of the star Sirius, which rises every 365 days near the sun.

The overarching time system of social life was organised around the categories of 'this' life (where we are now in the present); the fact of corporal death; and, most importantly, the afterlife. The concept of time in the afterlife included both the problematic of where or how the elite) will live in the future (largely as a disembodied entity in the sky), as well as its existence therefore as a parallel time which is continuous i.e., the afterlife is also an on-going stream of consciousness in which other kinds of entities dwell. Social life was organised around the assumption of a largely unchanging brief present followed by main course of eternity and was geared to the needs of the elite to ensure its place. Much of the industry and activity of Egyptian society was performed in order to create the future, and ancient Egyptian society invested a greater proportion of its wealth than any other (Redford 2003).

For much of the time of the Ancient Egyptian civilisation the afterlife was a privilege confined to the elite of the pharonic dynasties. The religious belief was that while all humans had a *ka* (a life force) which left the corpse upon death, initially pharaohs also had a *ba* (a special kind of life force made of distinguishing attributes) which remained attached to the body. The funeral practices were designed to free the *ba* so that it could be reunited with the *ka* from which point it could continue its energy as a new kind of intangible entity which lived in the stars (mainly) or occasionally in the West, behind the mountains near Luxor (Redford 2003). The *ba* returned to the body at night to regenerate, thus preservation of the body for eternity was essential.

The ritual opening of the corpse's mouth by the son to release the spirit was considered critical to the success of the journey to the afterlife. Initially this possibility was restricted to dynastic families and was therefore a privilege assigned to them as a sacred act. However, as the First Kingdom declined, the concept of the *ba* changed to include the possibility that other categories of humans might possess one, officials for example. Unlike the true elite however, officials could not become gods in the afterlife. Rather, they lived with their families and undertook activities such as hunting. Whether this was the case or not was determined by an act of weighing the heart (upon which all of the good and bad deeds were recorded) against a feather on a pair of golden scales The proliferation of social groups who could participate in such rituals also increased the probability that the corpse may not have a son to perform the opening of the mouth ritual, this being one of the key funeral rites (Smith 2009). In later dynasties, this duty was increasingly taken on by especially appointed officials in a system of institutionalised surrogacy which got around the problem of a lack of kin. These substitute systems for kin were to become an important aspect of ancient civilisations playing a contributory role to the development of administration and bureaucracies.

Tombs and pyramids, and other mortuary fortifications were meant to maximise protection from raiders as well as performing symbolic acts which expressed sacred myths. The construction of buildings commenced early in life and much of the activity surrounding the Pharaoh was connected to ensuring the future. In the dominant ideology the religious traditions and ritualistic character of society all point to the relative lack of importance of the present, which is positioned as a waiting room for the eternity of cosmic transcendence in the afterlife. The organisation of Ancient Egypt and its major industries were as much about the preservation of the future as attending to the needs of the present, which nonetheless were dealt with by an evolving and necessary agricultural and trading system. Art and writing originated in death rituals and the need to pass on mortuary practices. Advances in science, medicine and maths were explicable in terms of both the development of material systems such as rule, trade and money, and the social infrastructure needed to service and uphold the morass of contradictory, dominant ideologies which circulated until late in the Middle Kingdom. Hierarchies of gods were established, with the emergent concept of a unitary supreme being at its apex.

Lineage and the Tree Concept

A particular example of the use of the concept of generations which survived from ancient times through to modernity, and lives on in some forms today, is that of lineage i.e., the social task of providing a clearly articulated account of who is related to who by blood relationship, and thus providing an account of the transmission of rule. The Bible contains many examples of the use of the concept of generation and accounts of lineage for example in Genesis 5:1:

> Verse 1 This is the book of the generations of Adam. In the day that God created man, in the likeness of God made he him;
>
> … Verse 3 And Adam lived a hundred and thirty years, and begat a son in his own likeness, and after his image; and called his name Seth:
>
> … Verse 6 And Seth lived an hundred and five years, and begat Enos:
>
> … Verse 9 And Enos lived ninety years, and begat Cainan:
>
> … Verse 12 And Cainan lived seventy years and begat Mahalaleel.

However, accounts of lineage are performed according to key principles, for example, back through the line of the Father or back through the line of the Mother. The Bible most famously in the geneaology of Jesus Christ provides us an example of lineage difficulties. Presented in only two key passages in the Gospels

(Matthew 1:1–17 and Luke 3:23–28) the geneaololgical provenance of Christ differ, Matthew's lineage is set out via King David's son King Soloman and back to Abraham, and Luke via King David's son Nathan and back to Adam.

A critical challenge in the Biblical geneaological accounts, apart from translating time periods which do not map onto our own, is to deal with the fact of life of siblings i.e. that there may be multiple births each of whom may have claim to relationship, rights, status, the throne, power, inheritance, or in some other way disrupt the 'true' line of direct descent. Being able to demonstrate the antecedents and true descendents of Christ and the ability to demonstrate his connection to God, became ever more important in the Christian world, such that by the Middle Ages the authority of the Church and its agents was well established and had become codified into particular discourses and images.

Much of the imagery of the period has influenced our modern paradigms of generations and lineage including the concept of youthful generations and family trees. A popular and longstanding Christian image is that of the Tree of Jesse. Such images of trees typically show the ancestors of Christ, their inter-relationships, and their direct connection to God or his agents (such as Abraham). These images of the Tree of Jesse legitimate the line of Christ as the true son of God. The Tree of Jesse began to appear in Christian imagery around 1000/1100 AD (Watson 1934) and was popularised through the growth in illuminated manuscripts and the booming craft industries of the Middle Ages, which provided decorative opportunities in stained glass, stone work, paintings, tiling and textiles (see Male 1973; Reddish 2003).

Sources of these images included Psalters (Helsinger 1971) which were collections of biblical Psalms, other songs, and speeches were illustrated with the family tree of Christ. For example, Psalm 1 in the St. Omer Psalter in which the capital letter *B* (*B* stands for the Latin *Beatus vir*/ blessed the man), was decorated and updated by Humphrey Duke of Gloucester in the fifteenth century (British Library 2009).[1]

The textual basis of such illustration includes images such as that found in Isaiah Chapter 11 verse 1–3: And there shall come forth a shoot from the stump of Jesse and a root shall grow out of its roots.

The image of the family tree of Christ typically took the form of a central tree trunk at the top of which was Christ or an oversized Mary (Christ's Mother), with his ancestors arranged beneath him on a series of branches. The base of the tree with its roots was reserved for either God (as Jesse) or his agent (such as Adam), depending on the genealogical account given.

The images are typically in simple, often wavy and entwined branches made of plants, the tails of animals, plaques or banners which sprout from the central trunk. The earliest surviving window in the York Minster, York (United Kingdom), depicts

---

1   Modifying, updating or finishing a manuscript's decoration many years later was not at all uncommon at any period in the middle ages, rather like redecorating or remodelling a house. (British Library [2009] Psalm 1, St. Omer Psalter, online gallery).

figures sitting on the join of just two branches which meet, arc and re-connect. Other trees are much more complex with multiple branches, such as the elongated, ladder like structure found in Canterbury. The branches were adorned with God's gifts including characters from the Biblical 'begat' listings and the sacred (and indeed pagan) fruits, flowers, birds and animals of symbolic significance.

Deleuze and Guattari consider the lineage concept to be integral to a European paradigm, a function of a cultural imagination which is stuck within a paradigm of root, branch and tree, an arboreal imagination; 'The tree is already the image of the world ... the Tree or Root as an image, endlessly develops the law of the One that becomes Two, then the two that becomes four ...' (2002:5). The tree image produces unity in the most fragmented of social systems, organising relations into a meaningful continuity, in what is otherwise a discontinuous and meaningless flow of random persons who are born and die.

The tree paradigm of descent doesn't readily accommodate the appearance of the new and different, since 'Tree tracing' as a practice carries a logic of looking back at what has already passed, and tracing the lines of connection which connect the past to the present in continuous thread. The implication is that the past can never be re-invented, only copied in the relentless replication of tradition. In this sense, the past could be more than a guide to the present, and is rather a map of prescriptions for how things should be. Deleuze and Guattari (2002) however, wish to explain novelty by using a different image, that of the rhizome rather than tree. Rhizomatic shoots of life produce novelty in social life, generating materials from which a new assemblage (of all materials, spaces, ideas, and everything within the universe) might be created. We can use Deleuze and Guattari's (2002) rhizomatic imagery to understand prototype generativity, for example of inter-generational relations or of generational units where actors may gather and strike out in novel thoughts and deeds.

It is notable that in much of the tree imagery time flows from the base of the image upwards to Christ. The omnipresent figure was positioned at the peak of the symbolic hierarchy which in Christian culture was associated with the topside of imagery. Time thus flowed upwards, from the beginning of time to more recent time, moving through horizontal layers of generational descent. Alternative lineages which if followed would produce alternative candidates for the apex of the hierarchy are thus conveniently dealt with by rendering them as side shoots: their proximity indicates importance but substantially weakens their potential claim to the head of the apex.

These images are interesting for their other connotations, for example the concept of new growth and green shoots, where the Latin *virga* Jesus is the green shoot or broom of God, with the pagan associations of the green, Spring, new life, and perhaps an insight into the origins of the concept of the virginal Mother.

Perhaps most interesting of all for this book is the way in which the tree of Christ was to become adapted to provide accounts of family descent in general, beginning with the royalty and nobility of the day. Thus family trees of royalty emerged, showing the connection between the monarch and godly presences, as well as between the monarch of the time and their line of descent. Their siblings and cousins (potential competitive threats to throne and glory) were appropriately sidelined either side along the boughs. Early depictions of royalty and trees also showed the link between the head of the family, ancestors, saints and sometimes famous or heroic cousins even if somewhat distantly related in blood.

The general development of figurative imagery is mapped out in the unfolding journey of the tree image through the passing centuries. Depictions of faces or human figures are soon to be found perched upon the branches first complementing and then replacing the sublime blossom of flower cups and graceful fauna which had appeared before. In keeping with the emerging artwork of the painterly culture which developed in the West, figures in turn became more specific and personalised, representing firstly roles then characters or persons, gradually developing specific facial characteristics and even expressions of emotion.

The Time of Personhood

The development of images of persons and the concept of their descent through traceable lineages expressed a changing social concept of the human universe which became characterised by a growing self awareness and the development of the modern concept of personhood and 'people'. The individual awareness of personhood and the subsequent splitting and creation of the category of collective and shared (the 'We') are cultural concepts of self which can carry a temporal quality.

The awareness of time is itself cultural, in the sense that while all humans may share a concept of the possibility of change how this is constructed varies with historical and cultural context. For example, the concepts of both finitude and the after-life address the fact of the death of the body. The concept of a society which pre-exists and outlives us i.e., the social stream with its continuity of history unaffected by our birth, life and death, are relatively 'modern' thoughts of the last, say, 2,000 years, with modernity (the last 250 years) producing significant drivers which hastened its development.

The transition in cultural terms is the rise in importance of the concept of an individual person or self, which places humanity and its ego at the centre of the universe with the sense of time sliding towards the present, where we (at the centre of the present) become increasingly orientated to a past understood increasingly to be special and historical, and leading to us. This creation of a history which could be periodised opened up new ways of thinking about ourselves, including collective concepts where the shared experience is the time or times in which we live. The concept of generation carries a particular concept of self which is both collective, and temporal. Generation allows us to locate ourselves in dual time – a here and now which the collective shares located in a sequence of generations which happen before and after us in the all-time 'forever' of the World.

These ideas of lifecourse and life cycle articulate an old idea, argued by Mauss (1985) to be a category of the human mind, that of personhood. For Mauss, human personhood articulates an experiential awareness of embodied separateness which became '… over less than one and a half centuries, the "category" of "self" (*moi*)' (1985:20), a critical element of which was its capacity to be self conscious.

Mauss identifies the journey to modern personhood as moving through masquerade and a culture of masks, from personages (a form of role), to a named, unique individual whose consciousness and reason becomes located within the ever decreasing circles of their unique 'self'. In his discussion, Mauss provides what is implicitly a chronologically based, historical development of personhood thought to arise through different forms of society, from tribal to modern. Allen in the same volume draws attention to the eurocentrism of this evolutionist view which is 'an unhappy one … still understood as connoting the speculations, dogmatism and complacency of nineteenth century theorists' (1985:27). Since in practice the different forms of personhood co-exist in time (i.e., the mask is not ancient and primitive but continues in the present), we can view the lifecourse as borrowing elements of all of the 'stages' of development in personhood. Thus, the concept of personhood is an unstable category, and prone to changes of meaning and form in different social environments.

The emergence of personhood and the modern concept of generations developed alongside a changing concept of, and orientation to, time. This concept of time was both more social and less spiritual than the Ancients concept, with the idea of a present, a past and a future. Explorations of time in human society suggest that there is considerable variation in orientation to time, and in the meanings attributed to it. Evans Pritchard's (1940) study of the Nuer found that time itself was regarded differently from that found in modern, industrialised societies. For example, it couldn't be spent or saved, and couldn't be used to progress towards something in the future. In this sense, time doesn't pass, but is conceptualised as a more cyclical system. Östor questions the value of such dichotomies '… as we shall see, all these kinds of time exist in both kinds of societies. The crucial question is what these times are all about in given contexts' (1993:4). As Östor explores, all concept of time are about the sense of self and corporal awareness as much as time as a unit or flow.

Gell (1992) also explores considerable diversity in the concept and social organisation of time in human society. He shows how time is a structuring system which can consist of several layers of organisation, manifested for example in the simultaneous use of different calendars (for example formally in Bali). Thus, even though clock time appears hegemonically universal and natural, we can deconstruct and socially locate it to understand that clock time is an artefact of industrialism (Adam 1990; Urry 1996), just as labour time was a creation of the capital labour relations (Marx and Engels 1976). The industrial concept of time was more linear and less cyclical than pre-modern time is thought to have been. Bound up in ideas progress of and implicitly accounting for change, time's arrow takes us forwards, intrinsically with a sense of a movement in or across space.

The time of industrial capital has been argued to have been in part a globalising, unifying project, at odds with lived experience and the actual calendars in use (Evans Pritchard 1940; Gell 1992; Urry 1996; May and Thrift 2001). Hareven (1982) proposes the parallel existence of industrial and family time, the rubric of which locates women in lives which are marked by conflicting needs which arise under each process. Even while the beat of time was mechanically created as an autonomous system of precision (Urry 1996), cultural meanings were stuck to it. Weber (1930) for example demonstrates the moral value of time manifested in the Protestant Work Ethic and the concept of idleness. Such systems for both giving meaning to, and controlling, time created classes of citizens subject to it, such as identified by Thompson (1967) who traced the journey by which workers came to live by, and be valued by, productive time.

Prior to industrialisation there is evidence that time counting was expressed through metaphors such as night and day, or the passing of the seasons, and that subjectivity was translated into material practices for example around death (as explored by Hallam and Hockey (2001). Dominant institutions of the day enabled the production of autonomous time and its internalisation, for example through the practices of the Church where the increasingly fetishised rituals of prayer and ceremony were conducted within, and as, a strict disciplinary structure of demarcated days, hours, segments (Stein 2001), its rituals governed by special texts such as the Horologion (or Book of Hours).

The Generation Concept Pre-Modernity

Two metaphors of particular interest came out of the fifteenth, sixteenth and seventeenth centuries: Firstly, lifecourse as nature, and secondly, the human life span as a passage of finite time which is expended. These combined to produce a model of the lifecourse as endowed with seasonality characterised for example by sequential phases (the green shoots of youth; the autumn of maturity and the nightshade of death). These concepts were overlaid with other meanings, for example, the lifecourse as being endowed with special properties, magical if not mystical or spiritual, for example the quest for redemption in religious views of the meaning of life; the acquisition of wisdom in more secular views; the concept of an individual journey or pilgrimage sometimes characterised by trials which must be passed.

Shakespeare articulates these contemporary ways of thinking about 'having a life' which moves through youth to old age. The next extract is a clear articulation of a prevalent metaphor, of the seven ages of man, to be found in the play *As You Like It*. It begins:

All the world's a stage
And all the men and women merely players;
They have their exits and their entrances;

And one man in his time plays many parts,
His acts being seven ages.

Shakespeare [printed 1623], Craig (1980)

The seven ages are the mewling and puking infant, the whining schoolboy, the
woeful lover, the bearded soldier, the plump justice, the lean and slipper'd sixth
age, and the second childishness of the last age, 'Sans teeth, sans eyes, sans taste,
sans everything' (ibid).

Sonnet 73, written when he was 45 years old (he died at 52), articulates the
metaphors of life, death, and the persistence of love in old age:

Sonnet 73

That time of year thou mayst in me behold
When yellow leaves, or none, or few, do hang
Upon those boughs which shake against the cold,
Bare ruined choirs, where late the sweet birds sing;
In me thou seest the twilight of such day
As after sunset fadeth in the west,
Which by and by black night doth take away,
Death's second self, that seals up all in rest;
In me thou seest the glowing of such fire
That on the ashes of his youth doth lie,
As the deathbed, whereon it must expire,
Consumed with that which it was nourished by;
This thou perceiv'st, which makes thy love more strong,
To love that well, which thou must leave ere long.

Shakespeare [1609], Craig (1980)

These two extracts can be argued to show several different dimensions of personhood
which held relevance for much of the time in which sociological and psychological
theory developed. However, viewing lifecourse in abstract universalises what in
practice is historically specific and contingent to the differently manifested and
located personages. The seven ages of man is a representation of a masculine
lifecourse and is located in a bourgeois class location. The calendars of women's
lives have been argued to be very different by feminist critiques. Claims by those
such as Davies (2001:137), that a 'linear conception of time is grounded in gendered
power relations, and in a discourse of masculinity' are explored by Leccardi (1996)
who suggests that women's experience of time is discontinuous and consists of
knitting and reconciling fragments of different kinds of time activity. This has
been argued by Hareven (1982) to be systematised into organised social systems
of industrial time, which stands specifically in opposition to family time.

We can say that the modern concept of the life span, and having a life to live in an active sense, is a peculiarly modern and western development (Ikels 1992; Hockey and James 2003). Beck (1992) considers that this to be one of the defining features of risk society. Reflexive modernisation has made individuals responsible for their own biographies in ways in which the more organised world of industrial society did not. Industrial society organised people into roles, whereas risk society requires flexibility and the capacity for rapid change.

Giddens (1991) has argued that modern society has produced increased reflexivity which has assumed an hegemonic dimension, where having a life, getting a life, and developing an active management of life as reflexive life projects (Giddens 1991) has become an unavoidable central pre-occupation and structuring system of the contemporary lifecourse. This is particular so in more economically developed countries, where traditional systems of kinship which defined personhood and relatedness are argued by Giddens to have become distended across time and space, and its hold to have waned.

Adam (1998) systemises a model of time as a structuring timescape, allowing us to think of time-within-time, generating time lags, accumulation, and incoherence. This contrasts with what Adam feels to be a largely hegemonic orientation to the time of the present and enables us to see the masks of the lifecourse as time-dependent. In contemporary western lifecourses where age has become the prism through which the human experience of time has become viewed (Hockey and James 2003) the masks have become masks of ageing, and this raises the issue of how the *rites de passage* (Van Gennep 1960) of contemporary life are managed (if performed at all), i.e. how we get from one stage to another and how we might identify such stages (if they exist).

Exploration of the masks of the lifecourse in relation to one another, have also revealed their contingent nature. Aries' (1959) exploration demonstrates the historically conditioned and culturally specific production of childhood. Pilcher and Wragg (1996) in their study of childhood when subject to the discourses of the New Right during the 1980s and 1990s in Britain, demonstrates the creation of childhood as vulnerable to '... a gallery of social demons: single mothers, absent fathers, muddle-headed social workers failing to detect abuse, drug pushers, paedophiles, "do-gooders" ... "trendy" teachers, doctors prescribing contraceptives ... media executives purveying violent and sexually explicit material, and so on' (ibid: 2).

Even so, childhood is argued to be still a neglected area of investigation, since it has often been explored as 'adulthood in waiting' rather than as an experience in its own right (Brannen and O'Brien 1995). This has been argued to be a problem possibly shared by those identified as ageing, similarly constructed as dependent and inactive, in a system which constructs 'adulthood' as the 'prime of life', a largely unquestioned high status role which plays a powerful shaping influence in the lives of children and the ageing (Hockey and James 1993). Such constructions set up problems for the creation of other age based social identities, such as that of youth, shown by Murdock and McCron (1998) as a historically conditioned concept, and by the Birmingham Centre for Cultural Studies as a lived experience constituted through particular class relations (Clark et al. 1998).

Pilcher et al. (2003) argues that the experiences of adulthood is also an under researched area, while Hockey and James (2003) comment that '... perhaps we know only relatively little about the variety of age-based identities which individuals *actually* take on across the course of their lives; and even less about how these identities are, *in practice*, made sense of by individuals in relation to the wider social and cultural norms of ageing' (2003:5).

These contexts are those of the rise of 'thirtysomething', a concept used variously and in an *ad hoc* way, in the media and in wider society, although much less within academe. Sheehy (1996), while not challenging a linear, phased model, argues that the lifecourse has in effect been pushed back by ten years at every stage in both Britain and America. This has meant that a period which she interprets to be a provisional adulthood occurs aged 18 to 30 years. Beyond this, there is the First Adulthood, which is the Age of Mastery (45 to 65 years old) and Second Adulthood, which is the Age of Integrity (65 to 85 years old).

The first half of the new lifecourse has now become broadly structured as:

- Tryout Twenties: A period of prolonged adolescence (which follows the initial foray into the adult world, Pulling Up Roots).
- Catch 30: Passage to the First Adulthood.
- The Turbulent Thirties: Age 35 – Inventory taking.
- Flourishing Forties: Early mid-life crisis, the 'Little death' of First Adulthood; true Middlescence.

Such a schema still smacks of the universalism of lifecourse models, but steps towards cultural and historical sensitivity through her argument that this re-phasing is a generational event, practiced by the boomer population in the West. Sheehy's interest in her wider work is in the female lifecourse. In sociological terms, her work (1991; 1996) can be read as an exploration of the social reaction to the changing experiences of womanhood since the Sixties.

This reflects a move within lifecourse studies over the years, towards linking the lifecourse to their network, cohort and generation, so that the contingency of lifecourse experience and its historical specificity can be reviewed. Work by those veering towards a view of individual as embedded in social networks, such as Bertaux (1981) and Elias (1985) show not only the inter-subjective experience, but also the material conditions which shape the qualities of our inter-relationships, and their historical character. It is a small but important step to then locate lives in cohorts simultaneously moving through lifecourse events and from there an even smaller step to cohorts which become self aware, and develop a view of themselves as sharing their existence as a unique and special generation.

We can now see why the temporal dimension of generations is a movable feast, given the discussion in this chapter. The meaning of time in generations has meant everything from a literal period of for example thirty years, to signify a period of time with attributes. Even recent work such as Sheehy's lifecycle expresses a further possible periodisation within the lifecourse: it has become common practice to mark the landmark birthdays (the 30, 40, 50 etc.), and to refer to categories of identities as 'thirtysomething' or 'fiftysomething' and to talk about Generation X, Y and its variations as distinctive youth cohorts. 'Generations' nowadays might refer to categories spaced by only ten or 15 years; they are as likely to be defined by social processes such as the media and fashion as family relationships and procreation or any religious or spiritual system of belief.

The Kinship Meaning of Generation: The Tree Revisited

The concept of generation is commonly attributed with two senses, that of a kinship meaning, and that of a socio-historical cohort based meaning. The concept of cohort can be distinguished from generation by the different process by which it is created (researcher versus the researched) and by the system of relatedness implied. The influence of generation and cohort on studies using primarily one or the other is strong, as is the double headed meaning of generation which may be used in an ad hoc way in various places. It is possible that the systems of relations to which all of such terms refer have themselves changed, which has compounded the problem. For example, the kinship model has been argued to have been replaced by the cohort model (or at least weakened and supplemented) under processes of the transitions to modernity, so that Giddens (1991) argues that the transition is so great that the old use of the concept of kinship generation is now defunct. However, there is plenty of on-going work in familial inter-generational relationships (such as Irwin 1999) which suggests the opposite. In general, we may say that the kinship version of generations came first, and that Mannheim's (1952) analysis picked up the extension of the term to refer to cohort based processes which emerged as part of modernity. As such, it is informed by aspects of the original idea.

The kinship definition of generations stresses the blood relationship and intermarriage, and is a defining system of lineage and descent. Ardner (1989) sees the concept of kinship as a form of recruitment theory which societies develop in order to accommodate newcomers. The system ensures that each person is defined as a particular *kind* of person, being born into a location within a map of relationships. In this sense, kinship systems are a world structure of consciousness which define relatedness and belonging, and thus bind and entwine us into networks of affinity defined as kinds of people like us. One of the markers of what makes people into a kind like us, is their location in time. Thus, relatedness is also a relationship in time, and the tree structure of descent allows us to bring together vertical and lateral systems of connection and to identify a variety of bases for our relationship.

Apart from this ideational view, other treatments of kinship have stressed its material mode of operation, for example, the edited collection by Arber and

Attias-Donfut (2000) which explores inter-generational relations highlight the diversity of kin relations and how these may be conceptualised to form a wider inter-generational structure of relations. Finch (1989) notably examined the interaction of kinship meanings and inter-generational transfer, seeing kin systems as mechanisms of exchange.

Strathern (1992) reminds us that kinship systems are culturally specific. Taking the English kinship system as an example, she argues it to be based on the concept of individualism. Its universe carries particular ideas about, for example, the uniqueness of persons and the relational meanings of surrogates and pets. Strathern (1992), building upon Lewis Henry Morgan's observations of the defining discourse of kinship (as explored by Trautmann 1987), sees a central importance placed upon the uniqueness of parents. Particular forms of address enable the activation of kinship (for example the title of the location in the kinship map states the relationship, as in grandfather, father, wife), and are governed by rules concerning their use (for example, formality versus informality).

I suggest that the words are used to denote degrees of relatedness in space (brother; half brother), and in time (child, grandfather, great grandfather). The quantity and quality of degree define the category to which a person belongs. In this sense, the titles of the locations are co-ordinates in a kinship map of timespace, which defines our persons as selves in relation to others. Like astronomical maps we can gaze upon kinship maps and 'read' the groupings and lines between them in their constellations. Rather like burning stars throw out their light for many years after their death by virtue of the pace of the speed of light, so our ancestors throw out their beam. These distant 'great-great-greats', with their relatives set along the branches either side are 'remembered' into the present by kinship maps, offering the potential solicitude of sentimental connection and material gain through the property system of inheritance and tax. Such family trees tell us many things, including who we are in relation to others in the temporal flow of the social stream.

While kin has been the major focus of anthropology, I suggest that a difficulty arises with a conceptualisation of generations as a kinship system solely defined by blood relationship, partly since it overlooks the importance of kith. The old English phrase is *kith* and kin. Kith refers to the wider social network of contemporaries with whom we have a synchronous relationship. Kith are in effect our cohort, kin are in effect our family, and as such carries a concept of ancestorhood, stretching across a diachronic axis. I suggest that kin has been privileged in anthropology at the expense of kith, which may reflect something of the bourgeois gaze of classical Anthropology. (Strathern [1992] does make the point that what is under discussion is the culture of the English middle class).

It is true to say that kinship systems carry internal rules which allow surrogacy and the accommodation of certain sorts of relationships. Strathern (1992) comments upon the capacity of the system to incorporate friends of the family, i.e. 'close' friends, as 'aunty', 'uncle', the system ultimately exists to define the parameters of the family. As such, it has been used to define an exclusive group. Even though the English system is particularly well placed to accommodate internal diversity (in which Strathern (ibid) locates the origins of British multiculturalism), it does not easily cope with alternative kinds of direct and indirect relationship such as friends, gangs, acquaintances, movements, associations, parties, unions, networks, colleagues, neighbourhoods, communities i.e. the kinds of relatedness which emerged through urbanisation and an industrial–capitalist mode of production. These forms of relatedness have all been prototype categories (Rosch and Lloyd 1978), which have transformed both kin and kith relations. The concepts of generation and cohorts have been used to articulate something of this social change in relatedness. Overlooking kith by privileging kin may play to dominant ideologies, rather than sociological truths. Perhaps a complementary explanation for the privileging of kinship over kith lies in the social tasks which kinship systems have so effectively managed: property, inheritance, and affinity which bequeathed obligation, responsibility and exchange; marriage and trading systems, arrangements of habitation, education, the care of the sick and disposal of the dead. Kith have been very useful to the survival of the human race, but the simple power of blood relationship and loyalty to the clan or tribe may have ensured its survival, rather than been merely useful.

Conclusion

The concept of generation has had a precarious existence prior to modernity. Its main showing as an actual concept in Ancient civilisations was as an image to indicate phases of time and the particular kinds of men who lived then. It demonstrated the connection of the present to the past, and thus always contained an idea of lineage and descent by individuals and cohorts. Changing concepts of time meant the development of a more closed meaning of generation, which acknowledges birth and death conducted in slices of time more clearly defined.

At its base, the concept of generation is largely one of co-existence and relatedness within a temporal dimension. In Ancient Egypt the social universe consists of a vast number of kinds of entities: humans, animals, gods, weather, stones, the sea, and so on, which co-existed in time split largely between the brief present and the eternal afterlife. Ancient Greek culture located humans in their interaction with the Gods with its own history through the ages. As a distinctively human and social concept of time developed, time and relatedness could be described in more than one dimension. The time of the social stream and eternity is for all time, whereas my 'own' local time of the individual person is small and largely inconsequential until gods or their descendents take on human form, and their lineage must be ascertained so that our relationships are clearly defined.

The chapter considered some of the ways in which this was addressed, looking at particular at the development of imagery of the Tree of Jesse in the West, which was, in due course, to be laterally applied to the family tree. As 'modern' individuals appeared, so did kinship maps producing identities and roles based on their location in their relational network at different moments in time as the relational network was replenished. While we cannot cease to be a sibling or someone's child, we can take on other roles such as becoming a parent or grandparent, which moves the kinship network around us. This also suggests that life may be lived in different phases, initially defined by our changing location to the newcomers to the kinship network. The emergence of persons with lives which can change is a short step. The modern concept of generation can be seen as an aggregation of this, an adding together of all of the offspring, located simultaneously in a slice of, by now sliceable, time.

Thinking about the generation concept through pre-modernity is challenging yet fruitful. The career of the concept shows us the changing conceptualisations and use of time and space, and asks us to reflect upon our human capacity to understand ourselves in both the plural (the 'We') and the singular (the 'I') simultaneously.

Chapter 2
Mannheim and the Modern Concept of Generation

Modernity and the 1914–18 War presented new opportunities for the concept of generation which became popularised, to refer to the mass, national mobilisations of epic generations. These are discussed further in Chapter 5, which explores the generation of 1914–18. However this chapter begins by situating Mannheim's intervention in the social and intellectual contexts of the nineteenth and early twentieth century. It was an age of change, when social concepts of time, space and the lifespan were radically altered. The concept of generation was found in scientific discourse; kinship and folk memory, or to narrowly refer to artistic circles and youth groups which had emerged in urban centres. The chapter explores the genaeological roots and intellectual strands of thinking with which Mannheim (1952) engaged in the *Essay on the Problem of Generations*. It was written as part of a wider work on the sociology of knowledge, and allowed Mannheim to consider the sources and drivers of new knowledge. *The Essay* allowed Mannheim to claim the problem of generations for sociology, not biology. He argued for an extra-familial and socio-historical concept where generations became both subject to, and the makers of, history.

Mannheim's Context: Time, Space and Human Ancestry

Modernity presented new drivers which led to a reinvention and adaptation of the concept of generation. These included:

Time and space The stretching of time through developments in nineteenth-century science on the one hand, and its shrinkage and unification by the widespread synchronisation of clocks and the development of technology such as post services and steam trains on the other, occurred as the World shrunk through travel, Empire and war.

Key scientific breakthroughs Including the popularisation and acceptance of Darwin's concept of descent and the significance of the rise in scientific discourse of the problem of kinship, relatedness, and descent and their deployment to conceptual frameworks such as nations, races and classes.

Discontinuity in the lifecourse   Industrialism, colonial expansion and mass migration produced discontinuity in lifecourses and thus sharp distinction in social experience between cohorts which contributed to the idea of social generations characterised by particular kinds of experiences, and theories of familial descent linked to nationhood. These were marked by a variety of practices from keeping family Bibles to making patchwork quilts and collecting photographs in the domestic realm and the rise of urban identification and socio-political and civic assembly in the public realm. Nations were extrapolations of the households in aggregate while monarchies provided royal role models of family life.

Youthful cohorts   Urbanisation, a new interest in youth, and innovative social analyses which sought to understand modern society, identified youthful cohorts (largely male) and other associational forms such as artist and writer circles and scientific cliques took on the nomenclature of generations.

Mass movements   The development of mass political and social movements from which grew new radical identities, and the increased attention paid to youth as a potentially powerful social force in politics and the state.

In terms of intellectual history and Mannheim's thought journey it is notable that the intellectual contexts of thinking about generations were themselves in a rapid state of flux for most if not all of Mannheim's life. Kern (2000:1) argues that between 1880–1914 there was '... a series of sweeping changes in technology and culture which created distinctive new modes of thinking about and experiencing of time and space', particularly in America and Europe. For example, prior to the late nineteenth century, there was no particular challenge to the concept that time was an homogeneous, steady flow which could be unitised and experienced as such. Social and intellectual changes both reinforced and challenged this. This culture was reinforced by the unification and synchronisation of the global empires and their infrastructures such as clocks, shipping, railway networks etc. Relatively simple devices such as timetables drove significant unification and synchronisation projects (see Urry 1996 for some excellent examples of this).

   However, I think we can argue that time was not merely synchronised. Culture was transformed by the effects of industrialism at the level of practice as well as institutions. These produced cultural ruptures in which the different times of day and the practices associated with them (working and holiday time; working and household time; the electrification of night time; the challenge to religious and ritualistic time) began to split apart. So I argue that we see both a synchronisation and unification at the official level *and* a splitting and compartmentalisation occurring at micro level of household, work, and everyday life. From a sociological perspective we can also note that modernity brought a step change in the concept of demarcated life stages, and that the time of life was apportioned (according to quite fixed social rules) to different kinds of activities defined by institutional systems (education; the labour market; the spread of official marriage, the general norm definitions of appropriate times to do certain things in life). The twin demarcations (social time and the demands of everyday life; and the lifespan) thus present difficulties in their largely irreconcilable demands (see Hareven 1982).[1] In the nineteenth and twentieth century we see further splitting, for example rural time with its cyclical needs of planting and harvesting which clashed with both industrial time and school time, requiring endless local adaptations to manage the heterogenous social time which had opened up.

We should not underestimate the intense interest in and awareness of these changes and the development of new questions about what it meant for concepts of self. In art and literature the passage of time and the awareness of social change was manifested in best-sellers such as Edward Bellamy's [1888] (1986) *Looking Backwards from 2000 to 1888* and H.G. Wells [1895] (2005) *The Time Machine*. Memory and identity became popularised and intellectualised: Marcel Proust wrote *Remembrance of Things Past* over at least ten years, publishing it shortly before he died in 1922. Writers looked to their increasingly personalised and individualised pasts (Kern 2000) understanding these to be specific and historical for example in the tradition of the Bildungsroman and its sub-genres (for example James Joyce, *A Portrait of the Artist as a Young Man*) at the high end. The proliferation of Dime novels in the US and penny dreadful in the UK, with their slim yet contemporary accounts of love, loss, murder and turpitude indicate a mass market with a largely unquenchable thirst for reading stories in which all human life is narrativised.

Time did not merely blossom, unify, split, speed up, and altogether transform in the present, the other dramatic change was its expansion. As Kern (2000) notes, throughout the nineteenth century the time of the Earth itself slid back, dragging the cultural conception of time and history with it:

- The Bible suggests that there was a Beginning.
- In 1654, Bishop Usher gave the year of creation as 4004 BC.
- In the 1770s the Comte de Buffon gave the age of Earth as 168,000 years old.
- In 1830 Charles Lyell gave a possibility of limitless time to allow for geology.
- In 1859 Charles Darwin gave hundreds of millions of years as a possible time of life on Earth (to accommodate his theory of slight variation).
- In 1862, Lord Kelvin gave parameters of between twenty million and one hundred million years as the age of the Earth (to accommodate the length of time it may have taken for the Earth to cool).

Yet time, space and distance were simultaneously overcome by the speed of the telegraph and mail; the possibility of travel; the synchronisation of time in regions of the World, and all the devices by which a transformation of time could be affected (see also Urry 1994).

---

1   The Seventies Feminist literature indicates among other things, the acute difficulties experienced by women in crossing from the family time zone to the labour market time zone, a difficulty which persists today.

Interestingly, the popular and scientific concept of generation not only survived these changes in how we think about time, space and history, but was boosted by them. How?

Firstly the expansion and speeding up of time changed the perspective on ancient generations, particularly the social understanding of their proximity. The 'discovery' of the great antiquity of life on Earth, and of Earth itself, in effect had a 'moving pavement' effect on the Ancient Greeks and Romans, who moved towards us as genesis moved further away. The truly ancient were to become located ultimately as Neanderthal man, and the antique generations of 'ancient' civilisations were to move closer to modern Europeans, sufficiently close in fact to allow new and sometimes romantic connecting lines to be drawn between them. Certainly close enough to boost the concepts of civilisation and nationhood as connecting to the present. The construction of ancient generations as of interest to the European gaze can be understood by relating colonial structures to travel and tourism. Furthermore, the opportunities for touring 'ancient Egypt' grew as businesses such as Thomas Cook's developed the tourist industry along the Nile. Cook's cruises of 1897 which could be taken in just twenty days of pre-organised and facilitated duration were a different prospect to the three month independent travel on local boats which had been the main avenue of travel as recently as 1847 (TIMEA 2009). Tourism particularly by French tourists at the turn of the century was popular, and was presented both in terms of the antiquities which could be seen, and offering an alternative winter holiday destination, as shown in the travel posters of the day ('Spend This Winter In Egypt Where A Perfect Climate Is To Be Obtained').

The opening up of Egypt and the invitation to gaze through Eurocentric (and Christianised) eyes coincided with the emergence of the construction of Egypt in particular ways through disciplines and institutions such as Egyptology (Zelik 2003 review of Reid). The interest in this and other civilisations contributed to what I argue to be the creation of antique generations: constructed as connected to Europe and yet somehow exotic these identities are marked by a proximity in space and a distance in time. The imagined connections sometimes literally expressed a colonial relationship (as in the case of France and Egypt) and sometimes a quasi-colonial relationship constructed through the status of southern Europe and Africa. Such antique generations are, like many antiques, valued not only in monetary terms but also for the identity conferred upon those who inherit as evidence of the connective relationship. Furthermore, such antique generations are endowed with attributes which constitute a legacy, the responsibility for the guardianship of which is held by the inheriting generation. Through these sorts of mechanisms, the 'civilizational inheritance' is brought into the present and connected to the contemporary generation.

Secondly, Darwin's theory of evolution, as an intellectual moment, could have threatened or even unseated the 'arborical' i.e. treelike concept of descent, changing the image of lineage through generations. The career of the concept of generations was somewhat boosted by Darwin and the scientific culture of its time.

The diagrammatic representation used by Darwin is similar to the medieval world of the Tree of Life, with branches and a central trunk which can be traced back to points of origin. Such images of descent have become commonplace and varieties of it have been used in discourses such as the 'family tree' as well as in the world of science and descriptions of families of animals and kinds of living entities (flora and fauna, for example). It was not really until the twentieth century and the working out of neurons, atoms and genetics that imagery became more diversified, still showing connections between entities but in a more random, less linear, and more complex way than the tree like structure allows.

Thirdly, while on the one hand, time and space was compressed and unified; on the other, time just seemed to fly by. The pace of modern life was increasingly contrasted with older, rural, peasant time, sometimes unfavourably (Kern 2000). A sentimental attachment to the world which was in the process of being lost and the inheritance from the antique generations (the remains of which could be viewed in situ via the Grand Tour) all boosted nineteenth century nationalism, and with it concepts of not only the national border as the natural border of the nation of related families, but in due course, the concept of families of nations. The cultural lens of tree-like connections, and the constellation of kinship relationships, far from threatened by social change, were useful vehicles for the expression of modern beliefs.

These discoveries and reinventions which gripped the culture raised important scientific questions about the nature of knowledge itself. What sense can be made of the undeniable fact that 'knowledge' does not only grow and deepen, but from time to time, itself actually change? Where does knowledge come from? The social origin of knowledge was a rich vein of philosophical speculation which Mannheim was to make his own.

Mannheim's Inheritance:
The Social Concept of Generations Pre-Mannheim

The concept of generations had become useful in academic thought prior to its incorporation into sociology by Mannheim in 1927. Wohl (1980:239) observes that when he (Wohl), came to write a history of the 1914 generation using contemporary social theory, there were four models available: literary generations; political generations; youth generations; and cohort theory. These were spread across the arts and humanities, and new fields in dialogue over the concept of scientific investigation. However, we should remember that Mannheim's *Essay on the Problem of Generations* was not translated until the early 1950s, and according to Murdock and McCron [1976] (1998) was virtually unknown before. Instead, we must look to a variety of streams of thought in order to understand the impact of Mannheim's *Essay* and its popularisation.

Turning to the particular trajectory in the analysis of literary generations, and in the arts (see for example Peterson 1930; Peyre 1948), this genre constructs gangs, circles, and schools, as providing an influential context for the production of successive waves of new creative work. In this sense, Ryder argues that this use of generations originated in alternative histories of the arts, '… in rebellion against the Procrustean frame of chronological sections favoured by conventional historians' (1985:11). Such a deployment points to the influence and role of the social network in which the artists and writers become situated. This is most clearly seen in Bourdieu's (1993) treatment of generations where he argues that the concept of generations arises in the field of cultural production where aesthetics begin to function under a model of what is, in effect, a model of permanent revolution.

Bourdieu suggests that modernity opened cultural work as a field. As such, it became a site of struggle between competing social interests, for example in the case of the arts, where the bourgeois class developed practices such as sponsorship and appreciation to secure status and position. The acquisition of cultural capital, for example the know-how of appreciating the old and/or new, drove aesthecised forms characterised by rapid change. Bourdieu suggested that this social circumstance favoured the appearance of 'new generations' every ten years.

Bourdieu considered that a power struggle is prone to break out between 'the consecrated *avant-garde* and the *avant garde*, the established figures and the newcomers … in short, between cultural orthodoxy and heresy' (1993:53). Writers, artists and their fellow travellers may group into networks, and acquire identity and the ability to reproduce their position in order to become dominant in their field rather than dominated by their field.

Randall Collins (1998) in his discussion of academic generational networks (constructed via the master–pupil [sic] and peer group relationship) describes these networks as clusters of emotional energy (EE) which he argues stimulate and maintain production. However, an important dimension of their social task is the production of a collective identity, for example in naming themselves, producing journals which attract a base of supporters, creating schools of thought identifiable with them, and so on. Such themes have been explored in *Homo Academicus* (Bourdieu 2001) where Bourdieu argues academe to also be a field and thus subject to the power struggles between such networks, whose ability to exercise the practices of cultural and social capital will determine the identity and position of the academic embedded within them.

Such work is notable in pointing up how conditions of rapid social change and the long term continuity of traditions might operationalise the concept of generations. For example, the classical traditions of art, literature, and academe can invoke the continuity of generations. Wisdom and authority confers value upon the aged, and the antique. Antiquity itself may confer a certain patina of awe upon old ideas rather as McCracken (1998) argues that patina to confer value on old objects. The Kings Library on display in the British Library, London, is a fusion of the two, the richly coloured tombs of ancient texts are set into the Kings Tower with its glass walls, to which visitors are brought around in groups to pay their respects to the antique volumes of old knowledge found therein.

The cross-over of the concept of generation from literature and art history into more sociological fields is an interesting one. Wohl's (1980) work is itself an example. His examination of youth in Europe between 1880–1914 explored a manifestation of generational activity which he argued took a particular form, finding expression as a literary generation, led or driven by the tragic soldiers recruited into the Great War of 1914–18. He uses the contemporaneous literature of generations at that time to understand the 1914–18 generation noting that sociological models at that time were largely informed by what was striving to be in a scientific model. Comte and Ferrari used the concept of generations in a positivist way, seeing the continuous flow of population turnover as driving social change, through creating a problem of integration and succession which produced opportunities for new ideas. Thus, Comte (1839) ascribed social change to the continual appearance of young cohorts, bringing with them a particular instinct, '*l'instinct d'innovation*', which would challenge '*l'instinct de conservation*' by which the older cohort were gripped. Even though empirical observations of change showed that change could change pace, a logical deduction was that change was brought by each new cohort.

A pre-occupation developed with the problem of the *spacing* of generations i.e. the timespan and borders of social generations (dismissed by Mannheim as a false problem). This was a logically interesting puzzle to solve, since, if it were true that each new generation 'caused' change, then to successfully quantify the period of time which elapsed between generations would enable the production of tables which would map the rise and fall of generations. This would allow the calculation of the law of (rhythmic) social change and change in the future could be predicted. I consider that this might be one of the genaeological roots of a persistent underlying concept in the generation concept, which implicitly imagines generations as *wave* like entities.

Theorists such as Mentre (1920) grappled with the erratic quality and occurrence of the waves of change, which he took to imply that the spacing of generations must be irregular. From this he inferred that some generations lay dormant, or consisted of the messy tails of previous generations and the forerunners of the next. This presented the problem to classical theory of why some generations might gain velocity while others did not. What conditions and which qualities would shape a generation's ability and likelihood to produce a wave like momentum of change became an interesting line of enquiry which has followed through to the present.

For Mentre the explanation lay in the distinction between generations in their culture and mentality. Generations could produce 'leaders', clusters of people who articulated and led the age. Mapping actors, groups, circles and networks on to chronological tables would reveal their dates of birth to cluster.

Dilthey offered a competing view of generations, in contrast looking to the meaning and qualities of time to understand generations, challenging the positivist view of time as external and objective, instead locating time in the internal and subjective world of mentality and feeling. This leads to a view that generations are a function of, and express, an interior time. Pinder and the *Zeitgeist* theorists explaining difference within one shared social moment as the outcome of different cohorts each of which developed different interior feelings of time. A stratified consciousness of time was thus possible. Each generation was launched into society which was undergoing a constant process of emergence and unfolding. Thus, every generation would logically develop its own personality or spirit, which was natural, and possibly mystical (with its own unique laws of development), through encountering its society.

This (according to Mannheim in 1952) essentially German and *romantic* approach didn't preclude speculation over the spacing issue, but opened up a possibility that 'contemporaneity was not a chronological fact but an identity of influences, an inner time that could be seized not by numbers but only through the insight of a historically oriented mind' (Wolf 1980:74).

Mannheim's Intervention: Essay on the Problem of Generations

Mannheim's insight in the *Essay on the Problem of Generations* (1952), was to gather together these strands of thought to show that the continuous social process was not shaped by innate, naturally occurring forces but by social and political processes. By extension, this applies to intellectual theories, ideas, and ideology, which Mannheim understood to be forms of situated knowledge (Coser 1971). Such self concepts which society generates were argued by Mannheim to emanate through the embeddedness of actors in the social process, and were largely the product of '… a co-operative process of group life in which everyone unfolds his knowledge within a framework of a common fate, a common activity, and the overcoming of common difficulties' (1936:26). His general theory of the sociology of knowledge was applied to generations in the essay (1952), in which he considered that he had successfully identified such a group process in the dynamics of generations.

Mannheim's argument rests upon the social fact that generations share '… a common location in the social and historical process, [which] thereby limit them to a specific range of potential experience, predisposing them for a certain characteristic mode of thought and experience, and a characteristic type of historically relevant action …' (1952:291). As such, generations share the capacity with other forms of social organisation such as movements, to develop thinking responses to their shared encounter with historical conditions. In line with his wider theory of knowledge which provides for historical and cultural relativism, based upon the concept that no actor can ever develop total but only partial understanding (Coser 1971) generations produced perspectival knowledge.

Mannheim suggests that a specific cause of intra-generational perspectival difference arise with different variables such as class, region, sex [sic], and language, which locate different sections of the cohort differently in the social stream and in relation to one another. As each cohort turns to face the social situation of their historical moment, they may work up their social materials in different ways, developing different strategic responses. Here he had in mind right or left wing radicalism in his contemporary social environment, and takes as his example the romantic and conservative youth versus the liberal and rationalistic youth in post revolutionary France which represent the 'two polar forms of the intellectual and social response to an historical stimulus experienced by all in common' (1952:291). However, this aspect of his essay is barely worked up in theoretical or empirical terms, the greater part of his interest lies in the capacity of generations to produce perspectivally differing social understandings as a general principle of a stratified consciousness between generations whose stratification of consciousness arises from the different relationship to and experience of the social situation which they encounter.

Mannheim's publication and its forerunner papers established the problem of generations in sociology. However, he was not the only theorist working on this problem at the time. Wohl's (1980) study shows the considerable interest which had developed around the concept of generation, and positions it as part of a wider social period of experimentation with social action and associational movements. Coser (1971) for example explains this in part by referring to Mannheim's own location in the Hungarian society. His early publications were sponsored by his peer group or circle of youthful academic friends, and as Wolff explains, '… in his first or second publication ("*Soul and Culture*") he spoke as a member, if not as the voice, of a generation in a more literal sense' (1993:2–3).

We can note here the importance attached to the moment of youth as the formative moment. Youth became a popular concept during Mannheim's time, although it is young *men* who are regarded as the generational actors who are placed to experience fresh contacts from assuming the roles of adulthood outside of the domestic and familial context. It is a short step from here to link the awakening of an individual to the rise of youth as a social force, and to base it upon a model of male adulthood. This viewing of a capacity of youth to act for itself bears a direct relationship to the rise of powerful social movements in the nineteenth and twentieth centuries, and to models of social and political forces in circulation at the time, such as the influence of Marxism (Coser 1971).

Wohl's (1980) study shows the importance attributed to the late nineteenth century phenomenon of gangs of youth appearing in urban centres, and how for example Ortega y Gasset deliberately set out to create a gang of contemporaries with a specific political agenda. The re-categorisation of the lifecourse stages was much in evidence during this time, a good example is found in Hall's (1904) book *Adolescence*, which Murdock and McCron claim was highly influential, 'Where Hall led, others quickly followed and built up an image of youth as a force for regeneration and renewal, bearing the torch of idealism and spirituality amidst the encircling gloom of rampant materialism' (1998:194).

According to Meja and Kettler (1993) Mannheim's essay *The Problem of Youth in Modern Society*, sees the power of youth as resting in the de-romanticised, sociological understanding of its lack of integration (its (as yet) undefined status and that the youth's own lack of social understanding of their situation is a direct outcome of the lack of sociology in the school curriculum). Youth therefore must make its transition, by becoming 'institutionalised'. This is particularly important in social formations where kinship systems have weakened and are no longer the basis of ascribed roles and relationships.

Don Jose Ortega y Gasset in Spain published his theory of generations in *The Task of Our Time* (1928) claiming that there were two kinds of social eras. A conservative era in which people felt a continuity with the past and thus continued traditions alternated with a radical era, an eliminatory or polemical time characterised by a push for change (Wohl 1980:140). Ortega y Gasset considered generations themselves to be a motor of history, calling 'the dynamic compromise between mass and individual the most important conception in history' (1933: 13–15). However, again we can see a familiar theme emerging, since Ortega y Gasset had also acquired a new associational network of young, male and activist orientated friends and acquaintances who dreamed in Madrid cafes of the social challenge which they might present to the stalemate of power relations in Spanish society at that time (Wohl 1980).

Hazlett (1998) suggests that generationalism in academic texts appears to have been in part a European matter prior to the Great Depression in America. He suggests that America produced no systematic generational theorists comparable to those found in Europe with the one exception of Randolph Bourne. In *Youth and Life* (1913), Bourne took a fairly conventional view of dual generation (i.e. the older one in power, the young lie in-waiting to succeed them), but placed greater emphasis on the process of 'succession', suggesting that the 'window of opportunity' available to each cohort was very narrow. Once past the age of 25, the ability to encounter new experiences would be severely limited, and thus the ability to both think and act outside of the existing frame, would be too limited. Bourne's perspectives can be seen to be very clearly influenced by a dominant concept of the lifecourse here, with limited life chances occurring once settlement in life had occurred, and perhaps even the expectation of a not particularly long life to follow (when compared to ageing societies today).

Thus we can say that the historically conditioned social life was assumed to be encountered outside of the home, as though the domestic, familial world were a historical, or even 'nature' incarnate. Women's generational formation and experience is marginalised and presents a special difficulty if women's roles are confined to the domestic. A difficulty with the trope arises if women's experience of 'going out into the world', was in practice, to be confined to the private or to return to the private upon marriage. Such a view can be extended further, for example to class analysis. The model of young man leaving home to enter the world and take his place, is a bourgeois perspective which does not make allowances for child labour, conscription or those sent to live and work in service.

Mannheim (1952) argues that generations develop a social life which is above and beyond the biological rhythm of social replacement. At its heart lay generational consciousness, which is at once collective, historical and socially aware of its location, i.e. it is a critical consciousness. Mannheim argued that this arose from the difficulties that each new generation would experience as they encountered the ill-fitting traditions and patterns of behaviour of their age. In recognising these issues as social rather than personal issues, cohort agents would work up the materials of their lives to become reflexive, knowing actors acting upon structure with intention. Diversity, expressed through generational units, might occur, with some actors working for the status quo while others sought to change it. However, what precisely a generation can be said to be, is defined in part by what it is not. In particular, a generation must be distinguished from concrete *groups* such as communities, which can only exist where 'members have concrete knowledge of each other' (ibid), and *associational organisations*, 'formed for a specific purpose ... characterized by a deliberate act of foundation, written statues, and a machinery for dissolving the organization' (Mannheim 1952:289).

This emphasis on consciousness and action is a major point of contrast with the classical view of cohorts as set out by Ryder (1965; 1985), who takes the view that 'The new cohorts provide the opportunity for social change to occur. They do not cause change; they permit it' (1985:11). Cohorts, made by researchers, live through the social situation which they encounter. Generations, made by actors, change the social situation even as they live it.

The role of consciousness is therefore paramount in generation theory. Mannheim (1952) understands consciousness to be in part a form of memory, where personally acquired memories arising from lived experience come to inform discussions and emergent social understandings of the present. Its narration is for Ricouer (1998) the means by which a continuous stream of history is made tangible, and comes to be present in the actors' social present. This is in keeping with a tradition of collective memory as Halbwachs (1992) described, rooted in Durkheim's (1954) concept of collective consciousness but distinguished by the specificity of collective ideas to particular communities. Rather than residing in an individual, it is a form of consciousness collectively produced and residing in the continuous inter-relationship of the social stream.

There is some evidence in studies of collective memory of its cohort or generation specific character and the longevity of such memory once formed, which has tended to provide evidence for Mannheim's argument. Scott and Zac (1992) explored generational memory by asking 600 adults in Britain to think of 'national or world events and changes' that have occurred over the past 60 years, identifying the most important. The Second World War and events in Europe dominated the responses. Importantly they found virtually no period effect (the most recent events e.g., the fall of the Berlin Wall in fact were cohort specific, to younger cohorts). The research found that the experiences of the formative years (during youth) were the most highly influential in determining which events people would select as important. Thus, in the youngest cohort, the moon landings were the most cited response, while television and jet planes were not thought as important. In looking at gender and class variables, the researchers found some evidence of gender difference in what was remembered, but this was restricted to references to war and the environment. In fact, cohort distinction comes out as the great definer once respondents were asked to rank items.

The specificity of memory to generation has also been found elsewhere. Schuman and Rieger's (1992) study which explored the social reaction to the USA bombing Iraq in 1991 (following the invasion of Kuwait by Iraq in August 1990), the impact of formative experience on behaviour and attitudes later in life are demonstrated. They found that the evaluation of bombing was made in the context of the particular war used as a reference point in comparison (the Second World War or Vietnam). The researchers asked their national sample which analogy they would use:

- Sadam Hussein of Iraq is like Adolf Hitler of Germany (and therefore this is a just war).
- Getting involved with Iraq is a lot like getting involved in Vietnam, and a small commitment at first can lead to years of conflict without clear results (1992:317).

Their findings were that the choice of analogy was cohort bound. However, the researchers considered this to be a cohort rather than generational effect, since the correlation with ensuing support or opposition for the war was very weak i.e., the analysis was cohort bound, but the position of support or opposition was divided.

However, I note that a criteria of generational effect set up by the researchers was of a widespread consensus across the generation in terms of response to the war: this does not allow for Mannheim's concept of generational units exemplified by the social response to the Vietnam war in the USA at the time which can be considered to have been drawn along quite tight generational unit boundaries (as explored by Turner in his treatment of the radical movements of the Sixties, which reveals both the radicalism *and* the conservatism present in the social response to inequality and war during that time). Thus, Mannheim's (1952) argument that an analysis may be shared, and reference points set up in youth may prevail, but that action taken on that basis will differ between units is shown by this study.

Conclusion

In summary, we can see that Mannheim pulled together diverse genaeological strands of intellectual thought about generations, making a key intervention which rescued it from both biology and an artistic or cultural reading, claiming it instead as a true problem for sociology. He argued that generations were largely youth based movements which formed upon the entry into wider society, upon which it encountered social problems which existing social scripts did not allow them to address. Their displacement from old structures afforded them opportunities for fresh contacts and allowed them to develop collective responses in order to find ways forwards. In doing this, each generation needed to develop its social understanding and could also develop a sense of themselves as an historical agent. Generations could become actualised, acting upon the social situation to make history.

However, while each generation is distinctive from its predecessors and successors, Mannheim also allowed for internal differentiation by the concept of generational units. These units, demarcated by a range of socio-demographic factors which included class, language and region, might develop a range of distinctive social analysis and responses. Thus, strategic responses might differ within a generation, not just between generations. Mannheim saw generations as bearing both reflexivity and social tasks, in this sense he created a modern twentieth century concept of generations. While this was found to have limits (which we will see in the next chapter), being largely confined to a model of young, male action upon leaving a family household, nonetheless, its richness of insight and set in the wider context of his sociology of knowledge leaves me in agreement with Pilcher's (1994) view that, essentially, we have an undervalued legacy in Mannheim's concept of generation.

Chapter 3
After Mannheim:
Lifecourse, Cohort, Generations

In this chapter we turn our attention to the three time-based, historicising concepts of lifecourse, cohort and generation. Frequently muddled, sometimes used interchangeably and all of them slippery in meaning, this family of concepts is mutually reinforcing and contradictory by turn. These concepts in part addresses the continuity of society given the continual replacement of its members through birth and death. In microcosm, we experience this as a sense of a continuous life (and continuous self) under conditions of apparent change. Ryder interprets the contemporaries, predecessors and successors of Schutz's (1967) formulation, as 'personnel replacement' (Ryder 1985:10). It is this 'demographic metabolism' (ibid) which produces the social task whereby each incoming group, characterised as 'the incessant invasion of barbarians' (ibid), have to be incorporated into the social stream.

Cohorts, like generations, are argued to be unique and unrepeatable entities since they are the product of the interaction between agent and structure which occurs. At every level of analysis, the individual, cohort, and generation are each thrown into history where they encounter the social structure and each other as constitutive of their lived experience. An explicit and important rule of the cluster's paradigm is that no unit can live outside of history, and none are beyond the reach of the relational system in which they become embedded. This incorporation is not conducted under circumstances of their own choosing. An important dimension to these 'circumstances' is the contingent presence and action of their contemporaries.

Lifecourse analysis, like cohort analysis, tends to chart a journey from point A to B. Subjects can be located in their historical moment by identifying the contexts of their cohort. It is in this sense that Pilcher (1995) identifies cohort analysis as one of four approaches to lifecourse analysis. The others are functionalist theory looking at the function of age; political economy looking at inequalities; and interpretative, looking at meanings of life. Generation analysis is similarly interested in how actors get from A to B. However, a much greater emphasis is placed on the process of understanding which is required to do so, and the collective's ability to take action which is informed by this understanding. The ability to develop the capacity for social action, which I will term the ability to develop velocity, is how a generation contributes to its historically conditioned social situation. Cohort analysis, while accepting the push of agency, skims the process of its conscious articulation and the long term consequences which arise from generation activity, in all its forms.

In terms of their place in academe, all three concepts (lifecourse, cohort and generation) are differently located between lay knowledge and expert systems. Whilst all are integrated into mainstream sociology, lifecourse has a much larger literature and has benefited from methodological innovation in biographical work, as well as developments in the expert systems of state which generate case histories and market, which produce audience niches with defined lifestyles.

The concept of cohort has been largely defined in terms of a methodological approach, with a focus upon particular issues, such as the problem of the identification of the parameters. It benefited from post war social planning and the state led production of social statistics, as well as from sociological and demographic trend analysis (Ryder 1985).

Of the three, the concept of generation is the least developed in a consistent way theoretically, and is not a mainstreamed concept in sociology. Its continued use by a lay public rather than in the social sciences is puzzling. However, it is my suggestion that firstly, the concept sits uncomfortably between the objective, positivist world of cohort analysis, and the subjective, interpretivist world of life histories, combining elements of both. Secondly, the nature of generational form has itself become pluralised to mean both a familial, kinship based system and a social or historical movement.

The Twentieth-Century Concepts of Life Cycle and Lifecourse

Glick's article *The Family Life Cycle*, published in the 1947 edition of American Sociological Review, examined the family as a social system. It can be located in a wider sociological interest in the social institution of the family and socialisation through which individuals live (interlinked) lifecourses. In the British case, it builds upon a tradition of work established by Rowntree who worked out how households found the means of subsistence at different stages of formation (Hockey and James 2003).

The concept of life cycle was further developed to become the more dynamic and socially constitutive concept of lifecourse, for example by Bryant (1987), in *Rethinking the Lifecycle*, and Hohn (1987). Allatt and Keil (1987) contrast the concepts of life cycle and lifecourse, arguing that the latter positions social actors in interaction with historically specific, social structures. Billington et al., suggest that 'while "cycle" implies a rigid set of transitions which determine the age-based status of the individual, "course" points towards the range of possibilities through which the individual negotiates their passage' (1998:59). Thus such work rejects the cyclical model in favour of nonlinear models characterised by a plurality of roles and directions.

Subsequently, some work has been devoted to considering the cultural specificity or ethnocentrism of the model, with important work by Ikels (1992) into cultural variation, and by Hockey and James (2003) into the diversification of the range of social identities which may be taken on across the lifecourse, given a wider context of individualisation and alternatives to the traditional family household formation. In particular, Hockey and James highlight age as a particularly significant institution, since it '… has become one of the key areas for the production of social identity, acting as a way to classify and order the passing of time in an individual's life' (2003:3). Featherstone and Hepworth (1991) rework the lifecourse as a post-modernised social institution, featuring a less linear-orientation to time and a greater fluidity of social identities, for example in old age (see Featherstone and Wernick 1995). The timespaces of the lifecourse can thus be recognised as subject to reinvention, for example in practices relating to death and memory (Hallam and Hockey 2001; Le Goff 1992), and in how we regard the times of our life as somehow 'different'.

The concept of individual which informed the life cycle/course model has a diverse genealogy including religious belief and practice (found in the Christian concept of the individual); cultural artefacts such as the modern novel with its *bildungsroman* form; the Enlightenment which constructed the '… individual as an actor independent of family or position' (Miller 2000:4); the rational sciences which grew through industrialism and colonialism (biology, psychology etc.), and social scientific concerns which initially solidified narratives of lifecourse, primarily through the concept of the life history into a 'complete' object in its own right (explored by Dilthey and Freud).

The post- Second World War turn towards planning and a greater use of social statistics and state sponsored research programmes based on quantitative techniques; radical social and intellectual movements such as feminism; and the postmodernism turn have all prompted a resurgence of interest in the lifecourse (Miller 2000), but it was more generally 'a confluence of movements in sociology and psychology in the 1960s [which] subsequently came to involve economists, anthropologists, historians, and others' (Kertzer 1991:18) which meant that the lifecourse has become narrativised as a journey of the self, which develops a specific, unique biography. This has included a model of a developing or accumulative self, found for example in the post war psychosocial work of Erikson's *Childhood and Society* (1977), and Levinson's et al., *The Seasons of a Man's Life* (1978).

Such models have been criticised for problems which 'lie in its universalistic, deterministic, asocial, and a historical tendencies' (Pilcher 1995:18). More recent alternatives such as that offered by Sheehy (1996) (working with a concept of crises as turning points which produce new passages) represent more culturally sensitive versions.

Such developments have been able to draw upon expert opinion developed through discourses of social institutions as diverse as medicine, the penal system, the military and education. These were important in the development of pathologised models of particular kinds of embodiment, which were thought to represent particular kinds of deviant lives, such as explored by Foucault in his study of the penal system (1979) and the history of sexuality (1981). I feel that one outcome is that lifecourses have been characterised as located in and of the individual and their body, and thus their responsibility and burden. Areas of expertise attached to specific parts of the whole were developed, splitting the parts further into smaller parts which became the object of increased surveillance (an example of which can be seen in the practice of phrenology). The growth of cases with records as well as expert systems of birth, death, tax and housing record keeping provide rich data on lived experience (Plummer 2001) and maintain discourses of deviance and thus institutional power (Foucault 1979; 1981).

The market has also produced its own expert opinion makers in the form of marketing, advertising and promotional schools of thought for example, which produce their own equivalent of ideal types of lifecourse (termed lifestyle) led by different *kinds* of individuals, leading different *kinds* of lives which can be grouped in systematic ways, for example through procedures such as segmentation exercises. Such techniques are now further refined, for example in the development of micromarketing and processes of customisation where strategies of one-to-one now exist (Kotler et al. 2002). This has been supported by the increased range, depth and rigour of market research and its capacity for innovation (Aakar et al. 1995). The data generated has sometimes been systemised into classificatory systems such as A Classification Of Residential Neighbourhoods (ACORN), developed by CACI Market Analysis Group as an alternative measure of socio-economic classification (CACI 1993). Even so, we should not assume that marketing analyses are necessarily in tune with claims to the postmodern found in social sciences and humanities. Some segmentation may adopt quite modernist frameworks (see Hockey and James 2003:192–3 for a discussion of the use of life stages by Mintel, for example).

In sociology, there has been the renewed methodological interest in different forms and materials for biographical works, such as documents (Plummer 2001), oral history (Thompson 1978), the use of life histories and stories (Miller 2000) and auto/biography (Stanley 1992), as well as the use of lifecourse data in models of psychological development, as explored for example by Stewart and Healy (1989).

In contemporary social theory, the transitions of modernity have been argued to have produced new sorts of biographies, detraditionalised and made flexible and mobile, where reflexive, individualised agents put together life narratives and navigate the situations which they encounter without a reference system based on tradition (see for example Beck 1992; Giddens 1991).

Cohorts and Coevalness

The literature generally treats cohort as a group, 'which may be defined as the aggregate of individuals (within same population definition) who experienced the same event within the same time interval' (Ryder 1985:12). In contrast, the lifecourse takes the individual as the unit of analysis. Cohort analysis starts at the macro, aggregative level and drills downwards into the specific careers of cohorts, whose membership is synchronised by their simultaneous exposure to lifecourse events (i.e., their coevalness).

Glenn (1977) and Ryder (1965) suggest that the concept of cohort originates with state processes in the Roman Empire, where the term '... referred to a Roman military unit, a common dictionary definition [being] 'a group of warriors or soldiers' (Glenn 1977:8). As with the concept of lifecourse, the concept of cohort developed through social institutions and lay fields of knowledge '... to refer to a person who is one's companion, accomplice, peer or associate, or in a collective sense, to a band or a group' (ibid: 8).

Glenn locates the emergence of formal cohort studies as being via '... demographers and for many years applied primarily to the study of fertility' (1977:7), which has meant in practice that cohorts have been defined by their birth years, as well as by *rites de passage* events such as marriage, retirement, and death.

Cohort analysis has been carried out in various fields, for example in studies of political beliefs and behaviour (Abramson 1974; Glenn and Grimes 1968), and can be used to isolate variables, as did Cumming and Henry's (1961) study of the effects of human ageing on the process of social disengagement, and Wright's (1991) study of the relationship between the size of the cohort (and thus supply of labour), and wage levels.

The concept of cohort has also been used as an organising principle in longitudinal research by centres dedicated to social trend analysis. Such research is relatively well funded, has a strong institutional base and thus protection over time, and generates archives which future researchers can mine.

An important British example is the cluster of studies at The Centre for Longitudinal Studies in the Institute of Education in London, which includes the *National Child Development Study* (NCDS) (the transitions of a March 1958 birth cohort); *The Millennium Cohort Study* (MCS), began in May 2001; and *The 1970 British Cohort Study* (BCS70). Further examples include the MRC National Survey of Health and Development (NSHD), and the ALSPAC cohort of 1990–1992 which tracks the 'Children of the Nineties'.

A major American example is that of the Michigan Survey Research Centre which conducted the *National Election Studies* between 1952–1974, repeating sets of questions relating to party identification and electoral behaviour every two years. Another data set lies with the archives of the Institute for Social Research at the University of Michigan (Glenn 1977). The development of opinion polls in the twentieth century have also provided data sets which can be organised around the principles of cohort, for example the archives of the Roper Public Opinion Research Centre in Massachusetts (which has collected all questions common to major surveys in America since 1936).

Ryder and Westoff argues that cohort analysis is based upon a particular model of the lifecourse, since implicitly, it '... presents life as a movement from amorphous plasticity through mature competence toward terminal rigidity' (1977:23), thus drawing our attention to a concept of youth as a malleable phase which is followed by an adulthood of congealed practices and encrusted values.

Integral to cohort analysis is the cohort's encounter with a historically conditioned social life. The cohort enters a pre-existing social stream from which it can never escape: 'The members of any cohort are entitled to participate in only one slice of life, their unique location in the stream of history. Because it embodies a temporarily specific version of the heritage, each cohort is differentiated from all others' (Ryder 1985:11). In effect, this means that each cohort develops what I have come think of as a unique and thus unrepeatable social life.

Primarily, cohort analysis is 'concerned with interdependencies between social change and population process …' (Ryder 1985:10), and is based upon a methodological paradigm of opening up a cohort, sometimes at periodic intervals, through which strategy the researcher can make generalisations about the state and operation of particular systems, structures, practices and processes as they impact upon the population.

While the concept of personhood runs through lifecourse and cohort theory, I suggest that cohort researchers view the aggregate as greater than the sum total of its parts. In effect, cohort studies produce attributes or identify characteristics of the cohort which lend them a kind of defining 'personality'. This personality is largely defined by the researcher (since the characteristics flow from the definition of the research question), but enables the production of distinctiveness between different communities in time. However, this in turn presents a methodological difficulty which we can think of as a smoothing over of irregularities of experience.

This is a general problem with categories where the flattening of experience means that difference becomes squeezed out to the margins or even disappears. Hastrup suggests that within categories '… there is no unity and strict symmetry. It is not all members of the category "bird" that are equally good examples of birds; sparrows are more representative of the category than ostriches …' (1995:30). Clusters of experience which become glossed and invisible could become disruptive to the category as a whole if recognised. Laufer and Bengston (1974) suggest that this is a particular problem which arises from quantitative aggregation which in generational analysis tends to smooth away difference between generational units, qualitatively different, for example in ideological structure.

This raises the issue of how new social categories arise as well as under what conditions they 'stick' and become stable. Firstly, understanding how generational labels, or identity locations might arise, Rosch and Lloyd (1978) suggest that there is a prototype effect. Defining a prototype as initially deviant and innovative, its arrival disrupts existing vocabularies of categories. The prototype therefore implicitly has to make a journey from outside to the inside of the register of meanings. Once brought into the general index of categories in circulation such prototypes develop into full blown categories. Hastrup (1995), comments upon the difficulties of identifying prototypes due to the multiplicity of processes which occur in category building. An example is stereotyping, where an entire category is represented by only one segment, and that segment is itself only partially represented. Thus, perhaps both generation and cohort analysis shares a problem of the successful identification of categories.

The Concepts of Cohorts and Generations Compared

Cohort analysis ultimately remains a creature of the researcher, who defines the cohort and develops its attributes or characteristics through the nature of the research question, Ryder (1965), Pilcher (1995), Miller (2000), Plummer (2001). In contrast, generation theory works with the subjective identification of actors, as well as their objective location. In this sense, generation approaches attempt a more holistic approach than cohort analysis tends to, although this increases the difficulties of carrying out such studies.

The concept of cohort offers the tantalising possibility of an organising concept through which we can think about agency and structure, in a dynamic, fluid and long-term time frame, a quality shared with that of the concept of generation. It is these shared qualities and an on-going debate as to the extent to which generations are really any less the creature of the researcher, which has produced a recurring conceptual difficulty, that is 'The term generation is sometimes used synonymously with birth cohort, or it may refer to a birth cohort with "natural" rather than arbitrary boundaries' (Glenn 1977:9). As such, the concept of generation is best understood as permanently unstable within disciplines and methodologies, as well as mutable in a wider context.

Comparing the concepts of generations and cohorts by positioning them at either end of a theoretical axis, while necessarily glossing internal theoretical debate, allows us to think through what kinds of social processes each concept address as well as what they share in common. Table 3.1 makes such a comparison. In social reality, some generations may be prompted by social systems such as institutional structures (for example High School classes in the US) while social action which 'seems' generational may in fact be more properly a period effect, and so on. Even so, such comparisons allow us to draw out the iterative relationship between agency and structure and to secure the concept of generation as an essentially sociological problem however contingent and messy when Mannheim's formulation is brought forwards.

Firstly, in cohort analysis the entry to, and exit from, the social process is identified by the researcher, who thus defines the time and the identity of the cohort (see Ryder 1965; Pilcher 1995; Miller 2000 and Plummer 2001). In this sense, they cannot be regarded as generations, *per se*, which in contrast is '... a cohort-group whose length approximates the span of a phase of life and whose boundaries are fixed by peer personality' (Strauss and Howe 1991:60). Beyond cultural identification, there is also the question of interests. Vincent for example suggests that 'A weak view of age strata would be simply that they are people in the same chronological age band: a strong view would be that they are people who have conflictual common interests over and against other age classes' (1995:7).

This leads towards a conflict model of generational relationships as Bourdieu (1984, 1993) proposed, and used by Edmunds and Turner (2002a; 2002b).

Table 3.1 The concepts of generations and cohorts compared

Generations	Cohorts
Are composed of groups with elastic boundaries and uncertain edges.	Fixed group boundaries.
Membership self-assigned and/or co-assigned by other generations. May/not be recognised by researchers.	Membership assigned by researcher and/or expert opinion. Cannot exist without others.
Internal difference the result of different strategies adopted to accommodate change: produces and are produced by generational units, which are a function of stratified consciousness and diverse social location.	Copes with internal difference by checking for key variables such as class, ethnic identity, sexuality, disability, gender, and their impact on the others.
May develop shared cultures and systems of identification; may include spaces and 'events' which become special, and are claimed as that generation's social territory: they are sites of action, and can become a structure of its own.	Cultural identification not crucial or even necessarily relevant to definition of cohort, which nonetheless may develop these, and become actualised. Upon actualisation, the cohort may more properly be regarded as having passed into a form of generation.
Constituted by its historical moment in a social stream, and by emerging consciousness of this socially interpreted and considered fact.	Constituted by research on the concept of (unchanging) clock time; calendar time; linear and modern.
Develops systems of memory, legends, artefacts, which are its 'own', these may/not be known to others, raising issues of communication and transfer, as well as collective privacy and collective consciousness.	Not necessary in the life of a cohort.
Familial and socio-historical generations and processes – at least two possible systems of (interconnected) generational affinity: individuals and groups share at least two generational locations, one in each kind.	Individuals are assigned to one key location and properly belong to one cohort.
May acquire velocity (and gain political power) or may be fragmented (and disempowered).	Cohorts are static in the sense that the boundaries are relatively fixed and its journey is paced (for example, the Class of 84 doesn't have the possibility of becoming the class of 86).
Produces debris: consumes its own and others' debris which become cultural and material resources for the acquisition of velocity.	Not as porous to flows of objects, memories, buildings, and other symbolic systems for example, music, imagery, artefacts etc, and might not have the capacity to produce large scale debris: may produce local and sub-cultural debris.

A defining quality may be to think of each generation as unrepeatable: cohorts are drawn up so that they are comparable, their distinguishing features of personality, specificity and uniqueness both created and erased by the tidy definition of the boundaries. What makes each generation unrepeatable is not only its own internal dynamic, but its inter-relationship with the wider generational web and the historical situation which it encounters. As it moves, it acts, and thus changes the social situation as it proceeds.

Post War Generational Theory

I suggest that we can think about the development of the concept of generations as moving along three broad avenues of exploration in the post war era which map on to the figure on page 2. In summary, these are:

Generation as social agency This conceptualisation focuses on an action approach to generations, typically seeing the wave like entry of each cohort to the system as generative of energy, combustion, change. This model tends to look for mobilisation along the C–D Axis (see Figure I.1, page 2) and its impact upon A–B structures. However, in practice movement in one may prompt movement in the other. For example, the two may be drawn into relations of conflict (as seen during the 1960s when C–D rose to challenge A–B) or relations of intense solidarity (as seen in the aftermath of 1914–18 when A–B reclaimed ownership of C–D).

Generation as inter-generational structure This conceptualisation takes all interaction between A–B in aggregate i.e., all structures A–B amassed, and seeks to grasp the flow of connections between them in the context of social change experienced (and sometimes driven by C–D activity). Thus, looking at how processes of transfers, obligations, reciprocity, exchange are structured both by systems of stratification and culture, critical social gerontology can connect gender change in A–B to activity along C–D and its long term impact on the inter-generational structure as a whole.

Generational map-making These maps show representations of society as consisting of a sequence of generations. These are usually shown to be exclusively C–D generational formations. An important component of their definition will be the regime or society through which they are constituted, and without which they cannot be constituted. Studies in this genre may not display a great interest in Axis A–B.

In practice the borders of such categorisations in theory are messy and porous, and so I argue for flexibility in such a typology. Nonetheless, it helps us to begin to unpack not only the different ways in which the generation concept has been deployed but the different kinds of actually existing generational formation and relationship in social life which it has been used to describe. Thus, none of the following three approaches are necessarily stronger or weaker *per se* as arguments of generation, but rather look through a series of different windows into the complex systems of generational structure and action.

Generation as Social Agency

The first approach, *Generation as Social Agency* concentrates on the actualisation of generations and subjectivity. This conception of generations is a model of high visibility and collective identity, alongside the politics of positionality which allow generations to become adversarial and possibly organised. Typically fixed upon the youthful moment, this approach will look for social agency, whether as social movements *per se* (for example Eisenstadt's (1956) study of the political role of youth movements in Israel and interwar Germany), or simply as self-conscious entities which exhibit practices such as evaluation and reflection, which in itself has been argued to be a form of generational action (Burnett 2005). This form of agency has been found for example by Andrews (1997) in her exploration of biographical narratives in reunified Germany, in which actors deployed the concept of generation to make sense of events in their lives and acted towards each other on this basis. It would be fair to say however, that the first interpretation (of generation as quasi-social movement) is more common. A recent example is that of the work of Bryan Turner (see for example Edmunds and Turner 2002a), which looks at the wave-like generational movements of protest from the 1960s and 1970s among others.

The events of the 1960s and 1970s undoubtedly boosted studies of generation and much was learned which has subsequently fed into youth studies. Exploring the experience of the post war Boomers we see in common accounts of the general trajectories of change experienced in conditions of affluence as well as abrupt disorganisation and deregulation. However, the impact at the level of the sociology of knowledge include insights such that the increased focus on a model of generations as conflict model based which '... became almost indiscriminately used in analyses of the student protest movements' (Laufer and Bengston 1974:181) can lead to 'cohort-centrism' as Wright (1995) termed it in analysis. Thus I see a tendency for a movement model of generational activism to become synonymous with generation theory for much of the postwar period. The influence of Sixties (and possibly also feminist) mobilisations on generational theory continue. This raises issues about the assumptions made about the nature of action of 'authentic' generations which influenced postwar social theory and studies of generations while also highlighting the rich vein of enquiry which generational activity provides.

These issues can be flushed out by considering Wyatt's (1993) useful typology of generations. Wyatt's analysis of the Sixties leads him to consider the circumstances under which a generation might emerge:

- a traumatic event has occurred (e.g. civil war etc.);
- heroes and/or leaders who challenge the status quo become visible and thus an available resource;
- a population growth or decline changes the inter-generational distribution of resources;
- privileged interval has occurred and generation enters a particular moment in cycles e.g., of boom and bust;
- creation of special memory which sustains collective identity and its stories or foundational myths;
- cohort membership provides subjective and material resources (e.g., identity; organisational sponsorship).

Such a typology contains some possibilities for generations in general. Nonetheless it defines generations as entities acting in a public arena, determined by economic, political and social cycles, and largely the product of 'big history'. However, big history comes in many forms, and the changing position of women does not readily 'fit' action models of generations, even though they have had profound consequences for different cohorts and produce generational identity and experience understood as such by actors at the level of subjectivity (see Burnett 2005).

Among the most sustained attempts at producing an action theory of generations is the study of the Sixties by Edmunds and Turner, who claim that '… the cultural history of the western world in the second half of the twentieth century is the legacy of this large, active and problematic generation' (2002a: ix). What we can learn from Turner's (1998; 2002a; 2002b) engagement with the concept of generation, in which he deploys Bourdieu's (1993) model of generation as a struggle between generations over control of resources (for example cultural capital in the field of academe), provides an insight into how generations may mobilise in a self conscious way. Using key concepts such as field and habitus, this enables the authors to demonstrate a theory of generations on a conflict model where the generation develops an oppositional consciousness to targeted groups lying elsewhere in society. However, building on previous work (Eyerman and Turner 1998), Turner's generational theory is based on a concept of social class which the authors suggest is an appropriate framework, given that 'By and large the concepts which surround the idea of social class may be directly appropriated by a sociology of generations, producing a range of notions such as generational conflict, generational mobility and generational ideologies' (Turner 1998:92).

Whereas class theory provides specific theories of class divisions the transfer of the class paradigm to the generation paradigm has smoothed away some of the finer points of generation theory. As Irwin observes, '… the processes seen to place generations in positions of mutual antagonisms are not clearly specified' (1996:305). Likewise, how or why culture is generated in practice, how for example memory may be actualised as political action, is not treated, but assumed.

A particular issue arises from Turner's position that 'One may conceptualise generational cultures in the same way as one now speaks about "class cultures" or "occupational cultures"' (1998:93). A critique must point up the difficulties of this given that Mannheim's (1952) theory of generation indicates that many different kinds of groups and associations might produce social understanding, including status groups, sects, occupational groups, schools, and movements (Mannheim 1936 and discussed in Kettler, Meja and Stehr 1984). To conflate sub-sections of generational culture with an entire generation is to rather assume an homogeneity of generation culture, and thus of action.

Rather than producing an homogeneity of culture, Mannheim both in the essay on generations, and in other work such as *Ideology and Utopia* (1936) pointed out the fragmented quality of culture, which arises due to the inability of any one social group to successfully grasp a social understanding of the whole in its totality. Group work is essential to this task which arises because individuals are embedded in the structure and within the historical process which they share with others. Thus, no group can develop total social understanding, and, as it is a social impossibility for all groups to share the same location, or to experience the same existential factors, all knowledge is thus perspectival (Coser 1971).

The work by Edmunds and Turner (2002a) is a notable contribution to the field, however the overly blunt use of a quasi-class theory and the adoption of Bourdieu's narrower use of the generation concept has led to a concentration on spectacular and masculine activity in the public realm which overlooks possible generational manifestations, for example on the part of women. Pilcher's (1998) study explores social life following a spectacular mobilisation. Three generations of inter-related women were interviewed regarding their perception and use of feminism and the change in gender roles. The findings were that the greatest importance of feminism was claimed by the youngest cohort.

These kinds of studies highlight the usefulness of situating a generation within its wider inter-generational structure. However, unlike the *Generational Map-Making* (see below) the authors bring together an objective identification of generational parameters with subjectivity.

Generation as Inter-Generational Social Structure

The second branch of post war generation theory, *Generation as Inter-Generational Social Structure*, concentrates on the structuring of generations and the flows of resources, obligations and affective meanings of inter-generational systems which in this framework is recognised as one of the key organising units in welfare capitalism. Thus, the relationship and cultures of and between generations which shape the tax, pension, education, health and care policies and systems, and in turn are shaped by them, is critical to our understanding of society. As such, there are a number of themes in this area of literature, including those rooted in long standing philosophical problems such as citizenship and contract theory. Take for example John Rawls (1971) work *Theory of Justice: Normative Ethics Right and Wrong* which considered the responsibilities to future generations of the current generations on the basis of the hypothetical contract we have with fellow humans in the future. This raises questions over the what kind of natural justice might prevail between generations which allows us to develop that concept of rights and move towards normative behaviour in the present where current generations have responsibilities of husbandry to ensure the future generations its right to life and citizenship.

This second trajectory of work around generations has been boosted in the wider social context of ageing societies, carrying with it important implications for the possible injustice between generations (for example see Korlikoff 1993; Bengston 1993 and their discussion of the rise of generational accounting and Laslett and Fishjkin 1992).

This has implications and consequences for public policy for example as explored in the special edition of the *International Journal of Sociology and Social Policy* (Mutchler 1997). In the EU, the ratio of the population aged 65 and over to the population as a whole continues to grow, rising from 15.4 per cent in 1995 to an anticipated 20.7 per cent in 2020; this change occurs differently across the various European societies. For example Ireland's population is expected to grow more quickly than in the UK (Concialdi 2000).

The development of the European social model (in which I am including the UK) after the Second World War institutionalised inter-generational transfers through the varieties of welfare capitalist models adopted (Esping Andersen 1996). In Britain, Beveridge famously invoked the concept of lifecourse – from the cradle to the grave – in the report on *Social Insurance and Allied Services* (1943), while continental European systems adopted solidaristic policy principles and structures.

Esping Andersen (1996) understands this shift to welfare capitalism in all its forms as a decommodification of labour, where dependency on income from paid work or unpaid work were either relieved or mediated to a greater or lesser extent in different models. Feminist critiques have focused upon the continuing relevance of the breadwinner model which positions women differently within regimes of decommodification, which has meant that welfare regimes have produced or reinforced gendered social divisions (Lewis 1993; Sainsbury 1994). The literature is generally agreed that the European welfare model is now challenged by the emergence of an ageing population. Reynaud (2000) suggests that the pension debate of recent has been as much connected to social change which challenges the shifts in the underlying assumptions of the system, such as the changing context of full employment and the feminisation of the workforce within gender (in)equality, as in fact to an actual crisis of pensions *per se*.

There has been speculation over the impact on the inter-generational dynamic of these changes, including the landmark study by Mangen et al. (1988), which conceptualised intergenerational relations on a three-generation model (older, youngest, and a 'pivot' generation in the middle). In spite of subsequent work in social gerontology, social policy, finance and economics, intergenerational transfers through the family was generally one of the less researched areas of social life until recently. There were notable exceptions, including Colin Bell's

(1968) study of the use made of mutual aid in middle class family networks, and the significance of geographical mobility to patterns of social mobility.

In theory, ageing is conceptualised as a system of stratification in its own right, where structural conflict might occur. However, research into subjectivity has found a culture of 'beneficence' instead (Dowd 1984). This presents a methodological issue, since at least some discussion of inter-generational conflict (see following) are operating at quite a high level of theoretical abstraction, sometimes losing the subjective experience of ageing. More subjective accounts might trap narratives of affectivity of individuals, rather than macro-conflict of which the actors may not be aware.

This raises the spectre of inter-generational struggle over resources conducted via the tax and pension system, following Rawl's (1971) discussion of social justice and inter-generational relations as a source of inequity. Arber (2000) suggests that the term inter-generational conflict originated in the USA (see also Preston 1984), and New Zealand (Thomson 1989). We can partly understand the seepage of the debate into European social policy due to the context of the wider crisis of the European social model, argued to be beyond its golden age, and thus struggling to accommodate and adapt to the new conditions of post Cold War, globalisation, demographic change, and flexible working patterns at a time when the inter-generational balance of tax paying and non tax paying population is changing (Esping Andersen 1996). As Reynaud explains, the 'colourful references to "demographic time bombs" and, more prosaically, to "the old age crisis" [is something of a misnomer, since] the overall climate determining the future of pensions is much more diversified …' (2000:3).

Concialdi points out that the inter-generational conflict debate is based on a particular dependency ratio, that of 'the *old age dependency ratio*, i.e. the ratio of old people to the working-age population … the most common ratio used in studies on the future financing of pensions' (2000:17). This is in contrast to 'the *demographic dependency ratio*, i.e. the ratio of non working-age population to the working-age population' (ibid) which provides for transfers to the young as well as the old. This ratio then 'gives a more accurate view of the economic consequences, for those in work, of future demographic changes' (ibid). Thus, the gender dynamic of labour market and education is equally important to birth rate debates, not least because of the caring deficit which emerges if the traditional division of labour between the sexes shifts, making it untenable to provide caring services to the elderly.

Arber and Attias-Donfut's (2000) finds no evidence to support generational conflict, rather more evidence to support the 'generational contract', as found and discussed by Bengston and Achebaum (1993), and Walker (1996), although Arber notes the extent to which this continues to be underpinned by the 'gender contract' (2000:2) by which she refers to the caring responsibilities carried out by the women in the pivot generation location.

Vincent's consideration of generational cycles of investment and disinvestment show the social consequences of the pension system as it operates across time, one of which is what he understands to have been 'pension fund capitalism' (2003:107) which 'appears to me to be a particularly pristine type of capitalism because of the enormous gulf between the apparent owners of "capital" – the beneficiaries – and those who actually control the funds, who in reality the fund managers' (ibid). Far from generations simply representing an inter-generational structure along which resources might/not flow, Vincent's conceptualisation is of a brave new world which is largely unaccountable and uncontrollable. I suggest that there may be considerable merits in considering a view of generations which stretches beyond conventional generation theory, and entwines into the global and local worlds of power within which all social relations are conducted in which the reality of finance is given equal attention to that of subjectivity.

Generational Map-Making

This third approach involves trying to map generations as a continuous sequence. Generational 'Maps' require a visual imagination in 3D to understand them. Flat on the page and typically represented in a tabular form, a succession of generations defined by their historical location or moment is displayed. Many are defined by their era, or more specifically, their interaction with the times in which they lived. The great and the good jostle with the tragic and oppressed like so many objects in a cabinet of curiosities.

The semiotics of such tables suggest order, a mathematical or at least a logical sociological imagination, and scientific objectivity. Rather as astronomers have mapped the constellations of the universe, so sociologists and historians have placed events and social actors in relation with each other in a constellation of generations which come to bear an almost quasi-astrological bundle of qualities or characteristics. (See for example, Strauss and Howe 1991 America; Cherrington 1997 China; Baker, Dalton and Hildebrandt 1981 West Germany; van den Broek's 1995 discussion of Becker's [1982; 1993] map making in the Netherlands, and Plummer's [2001] identification of Life Cohorts in Britain.)

In this field, map making is generally used to explore generations whose experience was decisively shaped by, and who in turn shaped, the major historical turns in the society. Thus there is a great emphasis on identifying and classifying the historically significant moments which we can conceptualise as turns. Examples can be found in studies of the Soviet Union in which historians and other social theorists linked the traditional form of periodisation by leadership to social cohorts, i.e. reading each succession of regime as a turn of history. Bauer's et al. (1960) study is an example, arguing that the distinctive generational experiences were produced by the shift from Leninism (and its reliance upon networks of 'old Bolsheviks'), to Stalinism (and its reliance upon 'modern technocrats').

The approach shares with cohort analysis a reliance upon the constructs of the researchers which the apparently objective representation doesn't readily disclose. Secondly, the methodologies used to draw up such tables may vary from researcher's expertise in the history of the society through to the use of interviews and life documents, which suggests considerable diversity within this approach, in terms of the status of the data which the tables constitute.

A more problematical weakness is the closed nature of the (social) universe produced. This tends to unify what might in practice be differentiated phenomena, as well as enclosing them into containers such as a national framework.

A good example of relatively extreme, unnuanced, generational map making is the Strauss and Howe (1991) study, *Generations*, in which:

> William Strauss and Neil Howe posit the history of America as a succession of generational biographies, beginning in 1584 and encompassing everyone through the children of today. Their bold theory is that each generation belongs to one of four types, and that these types repeat sequentially in a fixed pattern. The vision of Generations allows us to plot a recurring cycle in American history – a cycle of spiritual awakenings and secular crises – from the founding colonials through the present day and on into the next millennium. (Book jacket, Strauss and Howe 1991)

Strauss and Howe studied American history and distinguished a pattern of four types of generation, idealist, reactive, civic and adaptive, which repeat on a cyclical basis. This can be used to identify key trends of the future, as well as to distinguish between different sorts of social era, called 'social moments':

> A social moment is an era, typically lasting about a decade, when people perceive that historic events are radically altering their social environment.

> There are two types ... Secular Crises, when society focuses on reordering the outer world of institutions and public behaviour; and spiritual awakenings, when society focuses on changing the inner world of values and private behaviour. (Strauss and Howe 1991:70)

Here we can see the influence of classic ideas about generations, including Ortega's rotating social eras of regression and progressive possibility, and a claim of distinctive, almost astrological qualities of the different strata of generations. The study illustrates some of the difficulties of the approach. The closed universe on offer unifies the generational formations which have come and gone, and glosses inter and intra generational power struggles. The absence of African American experience is peculiar, not least given the call to generation and the mobilisation of generations as considered by Eyerman (2002) and Turner (2002) whose analysis of the Civil Rights movement and its unfolding into Black Power, places it as a central dynamic in America and international life during the Sixties. I suggest that the longer history of slavery and resistance could well be argued to map the American South with a particular generational complex in its own right. A linked problem is the overlooking of migration movements which present important generational issues such as inter relationship with indigenous systems and the distension of networks across space.

However, some map making is less closed and offers us strong sociological insights into how generational structures and cultures work over time, since rather than taking generations as a lateral slice of time, they show us how generations interrelate and unfold over time, breaking down the otherwise homogeneous generational universes on offer. It seems to me that this is the main benefit of this sort of approach.

This is particularly well illustrated by Hareven's study of two birth generation-cohorts (1910–1919 and 1920–1929). Born to one 'historic cohort that had migrated to Manchester to work in the Amoskeag Mills' (2000:145), the cohorts were split by the occurrence of the depression. Hareven (ibid) argues that the opportunities and constraints of the two groups are qualitatively different. They are made comparable by the 'before time period' and an 'after time period' (Edmunds and Turner 2002a:6). An important element in defining the study was to identify the historical situation through which the groups travelled. Hareven's study shows us something of the possibilities of a mixed generational-cohort analysis, in this case conducted by qualitative research, and the benefits of the skill of the researcher in drawing up the historical situation and locating generational sub-groupings within it.

Meanwhile, Cherrington's (1997) study of what she calls the Reform Generation in China explores diversity within generations and the nature of generational responses, by operationaising the idea of generational units, as well as mapping generations into a sequence defined by historical turns. She explains that previous Chinese sociology had distinguished between the university students, city youth (*chengshi qingnian*) and rural youth (*nongcun qingnian*). She claims that her own research, which relies on interviews of students drawn from a particular social class (young, and directly from senior middle school, not mature), were from a specific cluster of generational units and that 'Those not in higher education would form part of other generational units such as young workers (*gongren*) or young entrepreneurs (*getihu*)' (Cherrington 1997:310). Cherrington comments upon the difficulty of drawing generational boundaries across time or historical periods. Such boundaries, she acknowledges, are ragged in practice; she has needed to tidy them up in order to work with this model (ibid: 306).

Conclusion

This chapter has sought to disentangle the family of three time based, historicising concepts of lifecourse, cohort and generation, which seek to address the continuity of society in the face of the implacable fact of the death of the individuals of which society is composed. This constant 'personnel replacement' as Ryder (1985:10) terms it creates social systems of acculturation to manage social succession.

The chapter explored the differences between cohorts and generations, showing the first as the creature of the researchers and the latter as self-defined and active entities with ragged borders. The lifecourse meanwhile has itself undergone transformation which expresses to some extent and in particular ways the actual changing experience of the lifecourse as it is lived.

We next explored the genaeological strands of postwar generation theory noting that there were, for purposes of a convenient and perhaps overly tidy classification, three main categories. These were firstly *Generations as Social Agency*, *Generations as Inter-Generational Social Structure*, and finally *Generational Map-Making*. It was noted that the first kind of definition might suit particular kinds or manifestations of generational activity: this should not be subsumed into a general description of all generations, who if not fitting, might be then thought to not be behaving in an appropriately 'generational' manner. The first genre of action suited 'big picture' action rather than quiet and local change over long periods of time. The three categories showed the diversity of fields on which they play and the systems with which they interact in these different forms.

It was noted that the various locations of the three approaches on a diagram of generational structures as found in the figure on page 2 show us the richness and diversity of generational relationships while also allowing us to see the reiterative interaction between structure and agency. This leaves the generation concept as a highly interesting one for a wide range disciplinary styles of thought, sufficiently flexible for a wide ranging application, but having been improved from its rudimentary beginnings. However, it still leaves the generation concept in the lay systems of knowledge, and quiet what the future holds beyond the walls of academe for the concept, is quite another matter. This most reiterative of concepts might yet face fresh challenges along with its paradigmatic siblings of lifecourse and cohort, were there to be fresh waves of generational activity, which, wrought under different social circumstances, might yet produce new material to suggest a fourth trajectory of thought.

Chapter 4
The Epic Generation of 1914–1918

Between the 1850s and 1920 the concept of generation changed and blossomed in its social usage. As we have seen in Chapter 2 scientific advances including Darwin's theory of evolution and new thinking about time and space had coincided with the rise of a social concept of generation, moving away from familial to a cohort based sense of generations. However, this was still on a small scale and often limited to refer to literary circles, youthful societies and political clubs, or more generally 'the generations' as a sort of short-hand for talking about social continuity and change and to allow the enormity of recent discoveries (such as Darwin's theory of evolution) to be absorbed at the level of culture and knowledge.

The Great War of 1914–18 was to change that with the democratisation of the concept of generation both in its meaning and its widespread adoption and use. The period heralded the final demise of the pre-modern concept of generation which had been restricted to a family based, molecular model with the monarchy at its apex on the one hand, and its role in Christian belief on the other. But the Great War led to a widespread application of the concept to working class as well as upper class off-spring, albeit within the confines of paradigms of nationhood, and to a model of generations was a mass, national and historically significant cohorts firmly rooted in the social world. Finally, ordinary people could lay claim to a generation as their own in cultural formations of identification and belonging and work up the materials of their experiences into new ideas and knowledge about the world.

Thus the first half of the twentieth century saw the concept of a social generation change. I suggest that the 1914–18 youth generation became the first *people's* generation, and given its historical role can be understood as an exemplar of a new genre of generation spawned by twentieth century modernity, what I have called the *epic* generations.

This chapter explores the First World War generation. It produced what is sometimes referred to as the tragic generation (after Yeats); the lost generation; or the War generation. The first people's generation is marked by its epic activity and strength of specific, historical identity which continues today. This is in contrast to the antique generations of the nineteenth century imagined by religious guardians and the classical tradition, boosted in their significance by the intellectual contexts of the time.

After exploring the qualities of epic generations, I turn to the specificity of the generation in its social construction, looking at the role of memory and the interest in the mind; the cult of literature; institutions; bodies and sites of memory including a brief section on the Isonzo front in the Soca Valley, which provides insight into the national construction and orientation of the generation of 1914–18, one of the key qualities of these Epic Generations.

Epic Generations

I suggest that the first half of the twentieth century in particular saw the popularisation of the concept of social generation, which during this period came to represent an epic quality. In contrast to the antique generations of ancient civilisations, these epic generations were modern and tragic. Swept up in the social turmoil of the period, these generations entered societies which were traumatised and modernising. The generation of 1914–18 entered a world working through the first death throes of the nineteenth century phase of the industrial revolution, its modernisation and the by now visible and growing decline of rural life in Europe. Societies, states and empires were characterised by regime change, often violent, and the rise of mass society and expanding markets occurred in the contexts of economic instability with major booms and busts; the rise and fall of immense personal and family fortunes; and enduring poverty and hardship for much of the population stratified by brutally exploitative material relations.

The stories of the generations who experienced the turmoil of the first half of the twentieth century in Europe are at once both filmic and personalised. Within living memory and made real by a million narratives of every conceivable kind, we can touch and feel the people's history while sophisticated systems of inter-generational transmission has ensured that society is not yet ready to forget them.

Many of the qualities of social generations as assumed in generation theory in the social sciences and humanities are implicitly rooted in these epic generations. They can be characterised as famous, history making by adaptive responses and acting on the system they developed social identities which have been maintained after their death. Their stories offer a counterpoint to official histories. They offer personal and collective accounts (including those of particular generational units, to use Mannheim's term) which stand as counterpoints to the ubiquitous mythic narratives which surround them.

The consequence of the generationalism which surrounded the 1914–18 War was that the concept of generation was never quite the same again. The concept of generation became democratised, applied *en masse* to entire cohorts, generally (but not exclusively) defined by their youthful moment. This was nowhere more clearly seen than Britain. The identity and narratives surrounding the British Army on the Western Front (the British Expeditionary Force or BEF) acquired a velocity in magnitude matched only by French construction of its own tragic generation. Perhaps it is an irony that in Britain we are beseeched to 'never forget' the generation of 1914–18, since the over-riding social quality of their cultural *impresse*, is that they are largely unavoidable. The cultural space captured by the generation has been upheld by subsequent generations working with institutional memory systems of remembering. Perhaps they are doomed to the immortality which comes when society perfects its techniques of remembering (Connerton 2003).

The Social Characteristics of Epic Generations

History makers   The carriers of history, the mythic construction of these generations invite us to witness their social, but possibly doomed, task as they are set to work on spectacular projects of social transformation and resistance. This typically involves nothing less than war, revolution, rebellion, regime change, the establishment of a new society or resistance to such.

Modern and tragic   Constructed as modern and tragic, they present a doomed mixture of heroism and human weakness or even 'evil'. As such they tend to remind us of our humanity. This holds an enduring appeal, not least for a population which goes on to experience further wars in a wide range of theatres. Apart from anything else, this more or less ensures a certain reproduction and recycling of cultural texts about them at the level of popular culture (books; films; plays) and institutional structures (the education system; official memorialisation; the mass media and so on), since, if for no other reason, the commodification of their social identity presents significant market opportunities to a fascinated audience.

A national phenomenon   The generation may be constructed as a largely national phenomenon. In practice, it may have been largely assembled within national boundaries through national bureaucracies which hides its embeddedness within a global framework, with global inputs and consequences. Socially represented as being self contained and independent within units such as nation states and bits of empires.

Live in a mythic, total universe   The mythic universe of such generations is rich and dense in detail, it includes 'everything' from its physical surrounds and landscape, material objects, artefacts etc., through to forms of expression, language and art. It has favourite objects and sites of memory (Jay 1995) of special significance. As the universe breaks up debris is shed and left racketing around the universe of all generations. This can be re-assembled so that its debris hang like contrails over future generations.

Immediacy   We can touch, hear, see and feel the epic generation. They offer a form of vicarious 'I was there-ism'. Through their debris the coevals and the subsequent generations achieve a sense of them at work and play.

The state   Epic generations are thrown into specific relations to the state. It is both subject to its direction and can use it as a vehicle for its actualisation; it is also heavily dependent upon the state and civil society for its maintenance in memory and archiving activities are limited to the opportunity structures provided by it.

The 1914–18 War and the First People's Generation

According to Wohl 'A historical generation is not defined by its chronological limits or its borders. It is not a zone of dates; nor is it an army of contemporaries making its way across a territory of time. It is more like a magnetic field at the centre of which lies an experience or a series of experiences' (1980:210). So it has been shown to be by this first epic generation which set a cultural framework which was to dominate the interwar years, and to echo through the rest of the century. As Wohl remarks 'The strange mixture of idealism and biological determinism on which the generational interpretation was based ... [in] ... no way annuls the importance that this idea had in the history and consciousness of Europeans who lived during the first third of the twentieth century' (Wohl 1980:237). The magnetic field of the Great War generation was a function or expression of a configuration of social circumstances on the one hand, and the kinds of adaptive responses made on the other. The circumstances which allowed the generation to develop as such were that firstly the beginnings of war produced social change which was sudden and abrupt. The kind of war it was at the level of social organisation and technique was novel, and this alone produced novel experiences sufficient to show the inadequacy of existing social scripts. New understandings had to be developed, expectations changed, and emotion processed, in the rapidly changing circumstances in which the generation found itself.

Secondly, the war produced displacement, and thus the loosening of ties to home and tradition for both those who left home and those who didn't (for whom life was never the same again). For example, a recurring theme in the literature consistently shows the gap between the expectation, hope for, and even assumption of social continuity, and the actual experiences of the aftershocks of the War. This gap is such that the social experience of the actors is immediately discontinuous. The signs of disconjuncture are many and various including everything from the transformation of key elements of the class structure (such as the decline of the servant class) to the discourse of difficulties of 'adaption' and 'settling back down' after the war which many experienced.

Thirdly, the War also saw thousands thrown together, the displacement and re-concentration created excellent, fertile conditions for what Mannheim calls the opportunity to develop 'fresh contacts'. This arose in many arenas, including trench warfare; women providing services of all kinds; the arrangement of the war economy and changing governance structures of civil society; the mass movement of people; the development of alternative trade routes.

Finally, communication systems and a more literate population which had developed a tradition of writing; war communications including war reporting a powerful vehicle for propaganda and censorship (Zacher 2008); the role of the telegraph, and photography, leant an unprecedented immediacy to the war and introduced a vicarious drama to events, consumed by an increasingly avid and engaged audience of spectators. The war was played out in the public eye, and drew in unprecedented numbers of civilians and civil organisations, as well as military personnel and state bureaucracies.

The Magnetic Field: Creating the People's Generation

The magnetic field of the 1914–18 generation is constructed by a variety of mechanisms with various outcomes. This chapter is too limited a space to do justice to them, but rather selects some of the key mechanisms. Firstly, looking at the role of memory and the concept of the mind, noting that there was increased reflexivity during that period which allowed memory to be self consciously created and managed. Secondly, the chapter turns to the 'cult of literature' one of the key ways in which the War was recorded and the generation constructed. Thirdly, institutions of memory including the problem of corpses and the Missing, and the creation of sites of memory (Jay 1995).

The Mystery of Memory and the Mind

The Edwardian pursuit of progress was hastened by the Great War, which brought advances in every field. For example, the modernisation which had produced electrification, the telegraph, telephone and motor vehicles was boosted by the needs of thousands of troops and the efficient management of war. Invention and innovation was not limited to the material sciences: other fields of study were also boosted by the new opportunities in the aftermath of the War. Problems of the mind, such as memory and the unconscious were already the subject of intense interest, but the War gave new impetus to this field.

The theory and practice of psychiatry leapt ahead in response to a range to the impact of the war on individual soldiers and families. Novel experiences and conditions called for paradigmatic shifts. An example of this is W.H. Rivers' experiences at Craiglockhart War Hospital (dramatised in the third book of *The Regeneration Trilogy* by Pat Barker, *The Ghost Road* 2008) which led to his theory of the *Repression of War Experience*, published in a paper of that name in *The Lancet* (1918) (and remembered in a poem of the same title by Siegfried Sassoon). He noted repression to be in part the outcome of social relations in which relatives, medics and friends would urge the returning soldiers to recover by banishing the memory of war from their minds. Rivers, in contrast, favoured the facing of memory (albeit cautious and managed), recognising that recovery of mental health may rely on working through memory rather than repressing it. Indeed, working with memory could be understood as a technique for retrieving it which might be regarded as the principal problem for patients experiencing loss of identity, shellshock, and acute anxiety.

There was intense interest not only in memory as an object located in something mysterious called the mind, but also the actual practices of remembering in popular culture. This included the task of remembering family, history, lineage and generation, producing journals, keeping a commonplace book, maintaining the Family Bible, writing family histories and so on, as well as a rise in popularity of séances and an interest in spiritualism. Spiritualism was fuelled by the public conversions of Sir Arthur Conan Doyle and Sir Oliver Lodge (Jalland 1996) and provided reassurances to grieving families. The general trend was that societies for spiritualism doubled between 1913–1918 and peaked in the 1930s (Jalland 1996). Jalland sets this within a wider context of the decline of Christianity and its Victorian practices which had been towards personalisation and large funerals, both of which declined under the circumstances of the death of the War. Jalland thus argues that the practice of memory seen in association with the First World War can be understood as one of the practices of 'unbelievers'. This section of the population had been growing since Victorian times but was boosted by the War. Thus Jalland argues that the extensive practices of social memory which we see coming out of the Great War filled the gap left by the rise of secularism. In effect the institutionalised memory of the War dead was to use Jalland's concepts a form of 'civil religion' although as she notes the prolonged continuation of 'the cult of the dead' (1996:380) suggests this to have been inadequate.

The Cult of Literature: Writing and Language

This age of popular narratives through which the generation's identity was constructed and subsequently remembered as such was expressed in a range of forms including literary. The consequence of what Holmes (2005:xix) calls 'the literary cult' which developed around the War is that we tend to view it through its literature rather than its history. To some extent this has contributed to the mythic construction of what the War was really like. That this was a literary war has become a commonplace concept, leant strength by the outpouring of texts which we find particularly associated with it, and thus the generation of 1914–18.

A powerful source of imagery was provided by the literary poets, generally but not exclusively well educated young men who found themselves in the trenches and ill prepared for the experience. This group includes Wilfred Owen, Robert Graves, Siegfried Sassoon, and Rupert Brooke represented in collections such as *Poems of the Great War 1914–1918* (Penguin 1998) published to mark the eightieth anniversary of the armistice and taught as part of secondary school curricula. Some of the most acclaimed poetry came from youthful artists and writers of the time. An example is Anna Akhmatova, whose third book of poems *White Flock* contains the well known poem *In Memoriam, July 19, 1914*. Her despair over the War was captured neatly in another poem in the next collection *Plantain*, which begins:

> Why is this century worse than those others?
> Maybe, because, in sadness and alarm,

It only touched the blackest of the ulcers
And couldn't heal it in time.

(Akhmatova 2006:49)

To these we can add the large number of poets more generally and less famously who emerged during the War and its aftermath. This phenomenon was commented upon with some exasperation in the trench newspaper *The Wipers Times*, which relied on submissions from the soldiers on deployment, on the part of the editors of the fourth issue:

> We regret to announce that an insidious disease is affecting the Division, and the result is a hurricane of poetry. Subalterns have been seen with a notebook in one hand, and bombs in the other absently walking near the wire in deep communication with their muse. Even Quartermasters with "books, note, one" and "pencil, copying" break into song while arguing the point re: "boots, gum, thigh". The Editor would be obliged if a few of the poets would break into prose as the paper cannot live by poems alone. (*The Wipers Times* 1916, 1:4)

The writing of the time was not restricted to high literature. An associated phenomenon was the mass production of news and the rapid production of newspapers with their comment columns, features, spectacular if gruesome headlines, and the letters pages. Satirical commentary found in *Punch Magazine* was complemented by the in-jokes, news items and lamentations found in trench newspapers such as the *BEF Times*, which amalgamated several other papers such as *The Wipers Times* (see Brown 2008), and published in two separate editions after the end of the War as *The Better Times*. Now produced as a collection by one of its editors Lieutenant Colonal F.J. Roberts MC in 1930 (Roberts 1930), the audience for such material with its unique mixture of satire and news rapidly developed once it became evident that the war would not be over in six weeks. Its apparent hopelessness became one of the recurring themes for contributors especially post-1916 (Fussell 2000), not that that deterred the what I would call somewhat 'sub-cultural' form of its gallows humour which outsiders might find at least surprising (commented upon by Ian Hislop in his Foreword, see Brown 2008).

These texts, married with increasingly horrific newspaper accounts and official texts such as those found in instruction manuals for the BEF brought their own discourse. Paul Fussell argued that this is a break with the past, the decisive shift from feudal to modern warfare and the concept of war itself far removed from the gentlemen's codes of etiquette which had previously prevailed. Examples of changes in the language given by Fussell (2000:21–22) include from steed to horse; from peril to danger; from the battle field to the front; to perish became to die.

A recurrent theme in the literature of the War is the idea of the tragedy of youth, cut down in its prime on a foreign field. It was a short step to creating an epic generation. The idea that this was essentially a tragic generation was fuelled by several different sources, one of which was W.B. Yeats and the Rhymers' Club founded in 1890. Yeats later termed them the Tragic Generation, on account of their social failure to make something of themselves, in some cases compounded by the propensity to early death. The sociological contexts are that the opportunity structure available to the group differed to that in comparison to their parental generation who had been able to take advantage of the expansion of capitalism. On the other hand, the events afforded new opportunities for social connections and fresh encounters, albeit lived out afterwards in the contexts of the 1919 pandemic, urbanisation, and the Great Depression.

The disillusionment and tragedy of the war took hold in earnest once the war was over becoming constructed in some quarters as an anti war sentiment. This sense of the futility of war and a question mark over who could really be said to be the victors was heightened with the advent of the Great Depression. The returning heroes who soon found themselves selling their war medals and searching for work (Holmes 2005) were joined in their despair by the female population of widows and the unmarried, or as in the case of Vera Brittain, those who married for pity and duty since their original suitors were no longer available (Brittain 1933).

The audience for the public understanding of the need for collective and individual grief rapidly developed as the 1920s passed and the Great Depression developed. By 1930, the audience were ready for some of the great writing of the period. An example was Erich Remarque's *All Quiet on the Western Front*, [1929] (1996) which presents the unfolding tale of four classmates who accept their school teacher's exhortation to volunteer for the German Army. The book is remarkable for portraying the minutae and banality of soldiers at war, the operation of everyday life as much about obtaining rations, getting enough sleep, waiting for letters and suffering boredom as the sporadic, if risky, fighting. It is also interesting given Remarque's limited experience of the War, since he did not fight in the trenches '… was slightly wounded by shrapnel, and after the war was censured for posing as a decorated officer' (Holmes 2005:xix). The book was made into a film in 1930.

The cult of literature should not be underestimated since, as Wohl remarks, the army of veterans returning to live through the descent of the 1920s are constructed for us in part by that literature, 'We see them through the eyes of Remarque and Hemingway as a generation of men crippled, both physically and morally, by their service in the war' (Wohl 1980:223).

The 'cult of literature' has since widened and deepened to include historical analysis including battle literature in specialised series and a wide range of historical accounts, including classics such as for example the historians' 'how it happened' literature: A.J.P. Taylor's [1954] (1971) *Struggle for Mastery in Europe 1848–1918* and Barbara Tuchman's [1962] (2004) *The Guns of August*. These kinds of texts have been complemented by those of the formal institutions of War, such as museums, in everything from guides and historical pamphlets to book publications. The debates have raged ever since, for example, about the battle strategy. In summary, the war in Britain and France hinged on the two fronts of East and West. The decision to stay on the Western front as opposed to drawing opposing forces off elsewhere fuelled the construction of the futility of war both through the depression years of the Twenties and Thirties and later during the Sixties and Seventies which saw both the defence (Terraine 1963) and vilification (Taylor 1991) of the British high command strategy (Holmes 2005).

The other rich source of the cult of literature was life history writing, including memoirs, auto/biographical publications and testimonies, and the publication of diaries, letters, and journals. This powerful vein of memory and generational transmission has been boosted by making notable the oldest surviving war veterans, and their gradual passing in the last few years has prompted fresh attention by younger generations. As the number of survivors with direct experiences of the Great War began to decline so the contemporary fascination with their life history as well as their social history, grew. These celebrity veterans included Frank Buckles who died aged 107, the last remaining United Sates 'doughboy'. He outlived his fellow American Harry Landis who died aged 108 in 2008. The Europeans were Lazare Ponticelli (last of the French 'Poilu') who died aged 110, Frank Kunstler of the Austrian–Hungarian central powers aged 107 in 2008. The last surviving German veteran Erich Kaestner, died aged 107 in 2008. In 2009, one of the last of the British Tommies died, Harry Patch at 111 years old, and was briefly the oldest man in Europe. This leaves 'Jack' Babcock in Canada aged 109 and Charles Choules at 108, the last surviving British soldier who lives in Australia, hence the widely made ascribed status to Harry Patch as 'The Last Tommy' in British discourse and the TV programme of the same title.

The interest in such celebrity veterans is reflected in the veteran literature about the not so famous, which has been produced, largely since the war. These include biographies written by relatives of the deceased as well as accounts of particular battalions or theatres of war. This literature is large and variable, and is driven by a variety of dynamics, including the recovery of history and silenced voices (see Arthur 2004) and relatives near and distant. This latter is fuelled by the availability of the battlefields and their construction as museums and tourist sites, which allows for modern pilgramages to be undertaken. A good example of this genre is *Bringing Uncle Albert Home: A Soldier's Tale* by D.P. Whithorn (2003). The book jacket reads:

> Private Albert Turley was just an ordinary British soldier of the First World War. He died on the Somme for King and Country. He didn't win any medals for gallantry and has no known grave. Like thousands more soldiers whose names fill local war memorials the length of the country, he left neither letters nor diaries to tell his story.
>
> This book describes one man's determination to piece together the events that led to a distant relative's death in one of the most infamous battles of the

twentieth century. David Whithorn reconstructs Albert's active service with the 3rd battalion the Worcestershire Regiment. His painstaking search for traces of Albert in surviving records and histories culminated in a pilgrimage to the Somme hillside where Turley fell in August 1916. (Whithorn 2003: Book Jacket)

Institutions for Remembering

The legacy of national and civic pride expressed by its institutions – systems of remembering (Connerton 2003) were commandeered in favour of social remembering of the War long after it had ceased e.g., memorials and museums and cemeteries were quickly and well developed and placed in prominent positions such as Churches and town squares. The deployment of such memorials was comprehensive, from the simplest of the solitary war memorial in a rural village in France to epic monoliths such as Thiepval on the Somme; the Imperial War Museum in London; and the Australian War Memorial in Canberra. These institutions have endured, even though '… one view of their function was that they should remain open as war memorials until the last of the veterans of 'the war to end all war' had died, when their purpose would be at an end and they should close' (Badsey 2009:1). Far from closing they have been carefully maintained and over the intervening periods, considerable investments made in them. These have been supported by rituals such as remembrance ceremonies; modern day pilgrimages as edu-holidays; and the creation of further monuments including museums, as part of a more general museumification of the sites of the War.

The earliest monuments included street shrines in Britain, such as an east London street where 65 men had enlisted from forty houses (Holmes 2005:628) an act repeated in the erection of many different kinds of memorials throughout the Twenties and Thirties as communities struggled to reconcile the absence. This is highlighted by Connelly (2002), in particular its social orchestration by community leaders and their assemblies by planning and fundraising acts of memorial in the East End and the City of London. These included the ritual act of remembrance each year on Armistice day, mirrored in France where, as Nora (1997) observed, a war memorial was put up in every village. This establishes the war in national consciousness, a realm of memory which was perhaps the final destination of the French generation lost in Verdun. In sociological terms, we can conceptualise this as a form of gatekeeping for social memory, preserving and constructing memory through particular kinds of cultural filters appropriate to the specific community involved, mnemonic artefacts which local communities will have been able to 'read' and in so-doing, reconstruct their imagined community.

Bodies and Sites of Memory

One of the issues of the Great War, was the disposal of corpses and remains and how to manage the expectations and needs of the living for the numerous defined as Missing. The 'Missing' represented a particular issue, since the living still demanded a mourning point and displayed as much interest in visiting the battlegrounds as those with an actual destination cemetery to head for. A major category of body was the missing body. For this category, and to stand in for all of the dead, various state memorials were created, themed as the grave which is symbolic of the missing soldier although this also became 'the unknown soldier'. These can be found in various kinds of locations including official churches (for example, Westminster Abbey in London); battlegrounds (for example, Menin Gate, Ypres); by region or theatre of war (for example, the Basra Memorial, Iraq) and monuments especially created for the commemoration of the War dead in important towns or capital cities (such as the Arc de Triomphe in Paris, with the tomb of the unknown soldier originally from the First World War but now both Wars, placed in the basement with an eternal flame).

The Imperial War Graves Commission was initiated in 1915 with the responsibility for British and Commonwealth burials. The British Government's policy forbade repatriation of the body. France allowed the relatives to choose the place of burial. Initially marked with wooden crosses and using duck boarding as pathways, these sites gradually developed into well ordered cemeteries with full scale monuments and the addition of headstones later. Monuments included the huge *The Memorial to the Missing* at Thiepval on the Somme unveiled on 31st July 1932, and the *Cross of Sacrifice* erected at Tyne Cot near Passchendaele with the support of King George V following his visit in 1922. These were part of a general campaign of building works which included for example: the Ulster Tower in November 1921; the South African memorial unveiled at Delville Wood in October 1926; and the Newfoundland Memorial Park, purchased in 1921, opened in 1925, and designated a Canadian National Historic Site in 1997. Many such monuments have more recently been raised, such as the Welsh Dragon put up in the cemetery of the 38th Welsh Division at Mametz during the 1980s.

On other fronts alternative approaches were adopted reflecting institutional and cultural differences. The Isonzo valley (now in Slovenia) saw intense fighting between the Italian and Austro-Hungarian armies. Here, cemeteries have a different feel, the approach taken allows for natural decay within a context of care and maintenance. Although Isonzo as a site of memory can be generally compared with the Western front it lacks shops, cafes and museums to quite the same extent, although the simple car park and local map shouldn't be confused with a lack of memoralisation. The sites in Isonzo are well maintained, signposted, and easy to find, and thousands of visitors make the trek each year to do so.

Visiting and travel as a social practice reinforced these sites of memory. Voyages to battlefields and cemeteries and the tourist of historical site became known as Pilgrimages, and making a pilgrimage had become an established social practice by the 1920s.

The first company to run such trips was the Michelin Tyre Company, initially to the Somme (France) and Ypres (Belgium), and it was Michelin which published the first touring guide with photographs in 1919 (see Michelin 1919). The British Legion sponsored the most well attended trip on the tenth anniversary in 1928

(Budreau 2008). Cooks also ran tours. Thomas Cook had built up his travel company from a humble start offering charabanc day trips to the English working class. From here he had worked up to residential holidays, expanded into Europe and the 'Holy Land' and then the Grand Tour. By the turn of the century Cooks had gone world-wide, pioneering the American West as a holiday destination, alongside Egypt, Japan, South Africa and Australia.

The outbreak of war was sudden enough to see 6,000 British tourists stranded in Continental Europe (Brendon 1991:254) and the war itself was close to a disaster for the Cook travel company damaging markets, rendering destinations unreachable, and taking a thousand employees off into active service, of whom one in ten were not to return (ibid 1991:256–7). However, pilgrimages made by visitors to the battlefields and cemeteries of the dead (although in practice and depending on certain conditions to towns such as Albert or along the coast) became a new travel route (Lloyd 1998). The Cook company initially stepped back from running trips to the trenches during the war, but said 'When the war is over it will be different' (ibid 2005:255).

Burial arrangements for American soldiers were a difficulty, yet one of the critical mechanisms by which War commemoration was to be practiced (Budreau 2008). Following the end of the War, the American government asked the deceased's next of kin whether they wished burial to be either in the battlefield; or to return the body for burial in the home town; or to return it to Arlington National Cemetery, Virginia. To mark their bereavement, widows and mothers were urged to wear a special badge, a Gold Star, which appeared on armbands and flags. Various associations formed including the American War Mothers and the Gold Star Mothers.

Between 1930 and 1933, many of the women who had elected for burial at the battleground travelled on special pilgrimages to the site at a cost of five million dollars in total while 'ultimately seventy per cent of bodies were returned in a logistical nightmare … at a cost to the American government of nearly thirty million dollars' (Budreau 2008:378). Further, 'To ensure the success of this high-profile public relations venture, no detail was overlooked … the officer-in-charge was responsible for inspecting cabin assignments, table settings, and all equipment from coffins to deck chairs, blankets and cushions' (ibid: 399). Budreau argues that much of this activity occurred as a direct consequence of the women's groups lobbying and successful manipulation of resources such as politicians and the press. However, all of this was overshadowed by the War Department's plan for the racial segregation of the pilgrimages. Indeed, this and the Black community's protest '… though largely unknown today, prefigured the civil rights movement that would blossom decades later' (ibid: 399).

Managing the remains was not a practice left behind as the century progressed. To this day the problem of identifying and retrieving the remains continues. Visits to the sites of memory are sometimes followed up by retrieval and removals missions. A recent example is that of Private Steinberg, who was killed in action in 1916 at Beaumont Hamel and buried in a grave with a cross. This grave has since been located and the cross changed to a 'Star of David' in line with his brother's grave, was then rededicated in 2005 (as recorded by members of the Western Front Association [WFA] and a WWI enthusiast www.wwIbattlefields, 31/12/09).

The museumification of the sites is itself a notable mechanism by which memory has been institutionalised and the generation's identity maintained after its death. It thus ensures the recreation of memory and a sense of place in a region otherwise first devastated, rebuilt, and then hollowed out by a general decline in rural life, agriculture and modernisation which act to remove memory. Thus, the museumification of the Western Front compensates, in Ritter's (Korff et al. 1999) sense for the absence of memory created by the combination of War and twentieth century modernity and is for me an exemplar of Foucault's concept of a heterotopic space (1994). Indeed Foucault (1986) accorded a special significance to cemeteries as heterotopias containing death. The implication is that death should be so contained, otherwise it may leak out through illness and disease.

As hereotopic spaces the battlefields of the Western Front play both as a special place lifted out from the surrounding stream of on-going French life and assigned to the time of the 1914–18 War; universalises the experience of the time (a process to which the concept of there being a generation of 1914–18, itself a universalising concept, is a highly useful tool) and allows new time to enter, carried in by what are constructed as the generations of today. Thus the occupants of the site come from a variety of time zones and realm. Its various constituencies are of small business owners involved in the educational and holiday trade; the heritage industry; parties of school children; families, some with young children; the relatives; historians, amateur and professional; and official bureaucracies charged with maintaining the site.

We can see thus see important social process at work in the outdoor museum-cum-memorial of the Somme, but in the contexts of this book, also see that while the generation of 1914–18 is upheld and maintained by such a place, such a place also acts as their container.

The Isonzo Front: The Site of Memory in the Soca Valley

The Epic generation of 1914–18 fought on other fronts, such as Isonzo. The Soca river runs through a high sided valley which joins the Julian Alps to the Adriatic Sea, entwining what are now Slovenia and Italy. In the time of the War, this valley represented a natural border between the Austrian-Hungarian empire and Italy, and for various logistical reasons was one of only a very few places where the Italian army might consider an assault. Such an attempt presented major difficulties, not least the Alpine conditions and the considerable if not insurmountable advantage of height gained by whichever army could secure each height first. This tactical advantage was ultimately shown to be held by the Austrian–Hungarian army and a series of twelve battle campaigns were fought up and down the valley. After the War, the area was annexed to Italy, and there was then a new period of regulation as the fascist regime attempted to bring the population under its control, often brutally.

The battles of the Isonzo valley were among the most difficult and most desperate of the War, and have been remembered as such and made available to Western Europeans. For example, the battle of Caporetto (now called Kobarid and previously also Karfreit) was later the setting for Ernest Hemingway's book *Farewell to Arms*. The town has become the base for explorations of some of the major sites of the War which survive and in its own way, become museumfied and memoralised. The ways in which this has been achieved include the *Kobarid Historial Trail* which takes walkers around the remains of battlements and trenches built into the surrounding valley and hillsides, with optional trails over the mountains to associated sites.

However, the historical trail also leads walkers past a range of other historically significant sites including archaeological remains, and natural geological 'wonders'. The universe of the War is substantially weaker than that presented on the Western Front. It is also queered by the subsequent history of Fascism. In the town itself is to be found the part ossuary, part monumental memorial to the dead Italian force erected by Mussolini, its mournful, tuneless bell tolling each passing quarter of an hour as it has done without ceasing since 1945. This is in part a monument to the 1914–18 youth generation who are represented in the frieze of remarkably beautiful young men performing various heroic acts carved around its base. However, in the best tradition of a heterotopic space, it is also a memorial to Fascism, not in an heroic or celebratory sense but as a marker of acts of oppression, and its victims, which followed.

Kobarid has a small but important war museum. Its' aim:

> The Kobarid Museum is not a museum of war but of man and his distress. It is not a museum of victory and glory, of conquered and trampled flags, of conquering and revenge, of revanchism and national pride. At the forefront are men who aloud or to themselves, for themselves or for their fellow sufferers, in various languages of the world endlessly cried, "Damn all war!" In short, their curse captures the fundamental message of the Kobarid Museum, its success and justification and the necessity that it lives and evolves. (*Dr. Branko Marušič: Kobarid Museum – A Guide to the Museum*)

The museum contains relics such as costumes and a mountain hut in a quasi-folklore model of museums. It also contains a couple of rooms framed as special, containing as it does equipment including a display of armaments suitable for hand to hand fighting under the conditions of the terrain. These heavy iron knives, axes, cudgels and spikes with jagged edges etc. are laid out in cabinets. The rooms carry warnings as to their contents but are still interesting when contrasted to the rooms of the Western Front which have few such weapons on show and where the act of fighting is somewhat subterranean. In that respect, the Slovenian museum offers a different concept of what should be remembered and valued. There is also a collection of maps, diaries and accounts of different aspects of the war; and a memory room in which visitors and partners from around the World can leave mementos and comments.

In contrast to the BEF front with its extensive networks, museums and well trodden routes, I was interested to note that there was little evidence of a general engagement on the part of the British including; a lack of visits by British school children; there had never been a recorded visit by a British establishment figure since the museum's inception; texts in the museum bookshop and more generally are not available in English; it is not the subject of an extensive academic literature in English for a British audience outside of war studies and certain specialist literatures; however mementos and a literature in English exist and connections with the Commonwealth states were in evidence. The pattern of visiting, the stories told in the museum exhibition, and the appearance and the approach to the monumental and memorial ruins out in the field produced a site of memory comparable to the Western Front. In other words, it was the same but different.

Accounting for difference leads us to see the specificity of national affiliation and connection to the Great War in quite how it is subsequently remembered. Cultural differences also suggest interesting lines of inquiry into what is remembered, what is fore-grounded as appropriate to be remembered (i.e. the memory aspiration) and concepts of how this should be performed. Regime difference is also a major factor. The Slovenian state experienced a different set of relations in the Cold War from France and Belgium, and the systems of memory and forgetting, its prioritisation etc., are reflected in this. A class element to memory is thus also revealed. Perhaps the museumification of modernity is in part not just as function of lost identity but of states which create an accounting surplus, over which budget struggles can be fought and won for its allocation to this memory project rather than that.

Thus we can see that these sites of memory provide institutional mechanisms by which the War and its generation can be carried forwards. Comparing the Soca Valley with the Western Front lends some weight to Winter's (1995) argument that these are remembered in very specific ways, reflecting patterns of national memory of the experience and construction of the War according to the connection to it. Winter argues for a more international perspective and approach to be taken to the memory of the War, a view with which it is hard to disagree. However, I note that this is not how epic generations operate in our culture. The dominant ideological discourses and frameworks of twentieth century modernity do not allow for the adoption of all generations in an international arena in an interchangeable manner, but rather according to the allegiances of their time and according to systems of stratification which foreground some sections of the population rather than others.

Conclusion

In this chapter we have seen how the epic generation of 1914–18 is constructed in specific ways, orientated towards a mythological overarching narrative of the lost, tragic youth, with a possibly misguided elite staff while at the lower level comes historical specificity: this battle, in this place, which affected *that* town/ *this* community, in *these* particular ways.

The Generation of 1914–18 offer us examples of generational formations on the AB–CD axis (as discussed through the figure on page 2). The emergence of generational consciousness including social knowledge about War by the generation is an example of the lateral, cohort awareness. This is shown to be stratified by class, famously in the literature for example with the contrasts between the experiences of the Officer Class and working class youth, and between the experiences of men and women. There are some grounds to suggest evidence of generational units. However, the AB axis interacts with CD and it should be noted that much of the construction of the youthful generation was carried out by other generations. This was partly using a discourse of lateral generational formations an partly through the processes of grieving and anxiety through family and kinship networks and the disruption to both axes at the level of social organisation.

The twentieth century was to herald a transformation in the use of the concept of generation in both civil society and expert systems. The century opened, as we have seen, with a concept of generation which was located in descent but the imperial chapter of Empire and fierce competition had produced heightened interest in, and a proliferation of, ideologies of nationhood, nationalism and race. The Great War with modern warfare waged on an unprecedented scale was a shock for the Europeans. It was not to even waged far away in a colonised land but in the 'back yard'. It's proximity and sense of immediacy was amplified by modern developments such as the telegraph, the newspaper industry, photographs, motor vehicles, and the development of the bureaucratic authorities.

The systems of memory are so well developed and well resourced that the 1914–18 generation seem doomed to march on for a little longer, at least until the escalator of time produces something to overshadow and then replace them, when they will finally be pressed back into the fold of history from which they came. For now, the generation of 1914–18 remain stuck like insects in amber, forever young and suspended in their time and space.

The concept of generation changed through the experience of the Great War. It became democratised, to henceforth refer to all offspring of society, not an exclusive description of any particular family or household's kinship network. It now referred to the mass experience of ordinary people and became a shorthand to refer to cohorts which experienced particular kinds of historical events. Secondly, it became conclusively attached to youth, and described a specifically modern and tragic youth. The memory activities of the Twenties followed by the scarcity of the Great Depression in 1931 fuelled the flames of the narratives which surrounded the generation and produced ever greater resentment and bitterness at what was increasingly seen as a purposeless sacrifice, and a loss to society of a vigorous youth which might have been able to pull it back from the brink of the next war. Wherever some kind of truth might lie, we can conclude this chapter that Wohl's (1980) 'magnetic field' is alive and kicking and to this day, the concept of the generation of 1914–18 is still with us. Certainly, the concept of generation has never been the same again.

Chapter 5
The Boomers: The First Wave

In this chapter and the next, we turn to consider the postwar turn in generational style and form towards consumption generations. Unlike the epic generations of the first half of the twentieth century, the consumption generations were rebels initially lacking the causes of war, revolutionary movement or depression. They also lacked the kind of historical tasks which had characterised the struggle of the epic generations. Rather, their identity was made through the relations of consumption and developed using the opportunity structure which their size and scale presented. They became a substantial market – hungry for style and expression. Displacement and the opportunity for fresh contacts arose for some (largely but not exclusively middle class) first wave Boomers by virtue of expanded higher education opportunities; for others the vestigial structures of segregation and the compulsory assignment to social spaces shared by others with whom common cause was soon identified.

The post war generation grew up in a time characterised by economic growth and social change. The chapter explores how the Boomer generations were able to exploit the social opportunities, becoming, in contrast to the epic generations of the first half of the twentieth century, market generations characterised by consumption and style. The following chapter considers the diversity of experience in the Boomer generation concentrating on the first wave born between 1945–1960. The second wave born between 1958 through the 1960s are the subjects of the next chapter, their overlap in dates foregrounding the ragged borders which lie between the two waves, which in practice overlap at the level of cultural experiences and identity for which the tidy dates of borders do not allow. These two chapters do not consider the neighbouring generation such as Generation Y, who came to be 'twentynothing' (Williams, Coupland, Polwell, Sparks 1997) and were made in part through their youthful encounter with the displacement and fresh contacts presented by the rise of the opportunity structure of digital culture, globalisation and new formations of youth culture.

The Consumption Generations: The Boomers

In the aftermath of the Second World War, new youth cultures emerged. These were unlike those which had arisen before. They did not arise as artistic circles or sets preoccupied with a particular intellectual movement or concern. They were not displaced from home and brought together by war or depression, and had no obvious historical task to perform at the outset. However, the Fifties gave rise to popular media and novels which spoke to the youthful gangs which had arisen as society strove to 'get back to normal.' Partly through these, youth cultures became increasingly the folk devils and the source of moral panics about 'youth delinquency'. The cultural products of the time explored the tense relationship which began to develop between youth and the parental generation, for example films such as *Rebel Without a Cause* and *Blackboard Jungle*, both released in 1955. *Rebel Without a Cause* tells the tale of Jim Stark (played by James Dean). The film shows the life of high school gangs; competition between them including bullying; girl-boy relationships; a chickee run (a car race) which ends tragically; and various bad relationships between young people and the adults in their lives including parents and policemen most of whom do not measure up to the youth's (or wider society) expectation. The film was a huge success, partly perhaps due to the death of James Dean a month before its release, and partly because it spoke directly to young people, alienated from institutions and the parental generation.

Crowther's (1995) review in the *New York Times* articulated the reservations which many had about it, partly because of the violence and general 'delinquency' which was shown, but also because the underlying analysis appeared to point to the root of the problems lying in Jim Stark's family and the 'suffocating' nature of small town America with its institutions. Crowther, while recognising some of the merits of the film as its honesty and drama, is dismayed at the negative views of those other than the teenagers, concluding that the film has been 'harsh' for example on the local police force.

Writing of the subsequent films in what was to turn into a genre of youth gang films, Parales suggests that:

> Teenagers, as a distinct group, have provoked particular fear and bewilderment since the 1950s, when they were first recognized as a separate culture and (almost simultaneously) as a potential market for everything from hit singles to acne medication. Even before the baby boom swelled the teen-age population, post-war prosperity was keeping them in school longer, providing more leisure time and allowing more mobility – all, as some adults saw it, encouraging children in mindless pleasure-seeking and dangerous rowdiness. (Parales 1995:21)

The recognition of the importance of youth in more ways than one to post war European and American society is a critical one: youth were no longer merely the harbingers of a zestful force for the future, but also a market in their own right. Indeed, much of the appeal of films such as *Rebel Without a Cause* is the insight into the habitus of youth which the miniature (and idealised) period piece affords.

Youth cultures and a post-war baby boom were to produce a large generation with strong concepts of identity. The sociological explanations for this are many and varied, as are the ways in which the Boomers are constructed in the literature, as exclusively referring to the post-war peak in Europe and America, or referring to this alongside the second peak of the Boomers, the long wave throughout the

Fifties and Sixties. The generations of the post war world took on a different *modus operandi* than those previously. The relations of consumption rather than production were more important, allowing the development of easily purchased and adaptable style as well as providing different kinds of settings in which youth could play out its social life.

The Characteristics of Consumption Generations

A broad typology of consumption generations is offered here:

The criticality of market relations   The generation enters social formations characterised by the importance of market relations which thus provides one of the key opportunity structures for the generation.

Identity through market locations   Can make identity through markets and is not reliant on the state for sources of identity.

Use of markets for competitive advantage   The consumption location allows the generation to formulate perspectives on how it may gain competitive advantage or resist a deterioration to such, and uses the market to do so.

Inadequacy of existing scripts of poverty   Relationship to relative affluence and improved life chances prompt adaptive behaviour on the part of generations who otherwise encounter social scripts which provide extremity, poverty and survival cultures inappropriate to the social puzzles encountered: the scripts developed may express higher order values and aspirations and the behaviour is that of societies producing a surplus even to some extent, while the generation is stratified by class.

The mythic universe is characterised by style   As like other generations, consumption generations are productive of their mythic universe and will populate it with favourite objects and special places. Their place in the universe will in part be defined by historical significance defined by relevance, style, influence, and directional pull.

The absence of heroism   Consumption generations may seek heroic projects and acts but may not be able to either find or create them. However, like other generations, consumption generations develop special projects of social tasks defined as unique to them. These are not tragic.

Ephemeral memorialisation   These generations, like others, produce artefacts and institutional systems for its own memorialisation. The relationship to the market allows an extensive production of materials, but subsequent transformation or the break up of the universe releases a great deal of debris into the system. Much of this can't be, and isn't archived. Much of it is characterised by its mundane quality and an abundance of supply. Lacking both scarcity and value much of it is lost. Consumption generations are characterised by an ephemeral quality, both in terms of their impact, and in the kinds of material held within the system which is archived.

The connection between time and ephemerality   Consumption generations, like all, become aware of their historical moment but may develop a particular set of relations to time and thus develop a concept of their own ephemeral nature and activity. This may be expressed in all of the outlets possible (art, words, actions etc.) and critically, become part of the defining culture of such generations. Thus, unlike epic generations who carry concepts of historicism, the long term and even permanence, consumption generations understand their primary sign as here and now. Consumption generations flicker and flare in their fold of history.

Locating the Boomers in the Historical Stream

Location is central to Mannheim's formulation, since generational membership or formation is made primarily through 'the phenomenon of similar location ... in a social structure' (1952:290). It is location which shapes the entry point to, and subsequent passage through, the historically specific present and is a powerful influencing force on subjective experience. As such, the location was considered by Mannheim to condition the existential basis of knowledge (1952). Traditionally, generation theorists attach considerable significance to the transition during youth from family to public environment (the entry point), and thus regard location as the youthful position in the inter-generational structure. Here lies Mannheim's process by which individual and collective biographies of ageing become 'primary factors ... [in] the shaping of social interrelationships in their historic flux' (1952:290).

  Entering the social present for Mannheim was to become located in the historical present (which Mannheim regards as being in a state of flux). This is a political and social present, defined in the pre-feminist concept of a public arena which lies externally to the world of the family, household and community. Thus, generational location means primarily the location in the intergenerational structure, but we can only understand the significance of this by locating the generation in its socio-historical situation.

  A theoretical problem arises with Mannheim's formulation since it implicitly locates households and families in the personal and private realm of childhood, while the socio-historical situation which is entered is a code for 'external society', where for example, intellectual and political currents are at play. Mannheim thus implicitly constructs a model of youthful transition as a drive towards independence, out of and away from, family, parents and household and into 'society', this being a common construction both for his contemporaries. This apparent separation of the family and household from 'society' is an interesting one: perhaps what Mannheim really refers to is the changing relationship to family during the youthful moment.

The Social Situation Encountered: The First Wave of Boomers

In Roland Robertson's (1992) five phase periodisation of globalisation, the Boomer generation were born into the fourth phase of the struggle for hegemony, defined as the period 1925–69. This struggle is characterised by the rise of a supra-national organisational level in politics (which begins with the League of Nations and comes to include European integration). This shadows and connects with the rise of global capital with its increased enmeshing of states and markets. The supra-national level, it is suggested, was a system which provided containers by which competition between particular configurations of players could be limited and regulated. Robertson argues that a particular characteristic of the era is the further global institutionalisation of militarised relations. Finally, world citizenship emerges as a publicly available, contested category, and it is through such a dynamic that perhaps we can see some evidence for Beck's (1992) assertion that 'self confrontation' (at a social level) develops as an intrinsic feature of a reflexive modernisation.

However, in Robertson's (1992) schema a substantial section of the generation, the later Boomers, come of age during *The Uncertainty Phase* (1969–1992). Robertson's Uncertainty Phase is signalled by the success of space exploration which provides something close to a revelatory moment to the world's population who, in the process of seeing the world from a perspective in deep space, develop a more profound sense of themselves as part of one world, a global world. This rise of the concept of one-worldism (more recently a concept of the global), has various implications in Robertson's eyes including the popularisation of environmentalism, a generalised increased cultural awareness of 'how small the world really is', and a sense of connection and responsibility in citizenship.

Further shifts include renewed efforts to integrate state competition (I would take as examples here the rise of the European Union, and the removal of the 'evil empires' of the Cold War), against a backdrop of the rise of mass consumption, globalising culture and global capital. This period on the whole is generally represented as one of profound social change which, as Wohl suggests, is essential to '… the formation of a generational consciousness … [which] provides a sense of rupture with the past … that will later distinguish the members of a generation' (1980:210).

The social situation which the first wave of Boomers entered was largely overshadowed by the events of the Second World War and its consequences. Many of the generation grew up under initial conditions of scarcity and for the oldest boomers, while the War continued. This was a brief period in only the oldest of the Boomers' lives. However, many did grow up in households in which the parental and grand parental generations had experienced the Great War, the Depression years, and the upheaval of inter-war Europe.

The Europe of 1945 was characterised by major economic, social and political devastation (Edye and Lintner 1996). Nonetheless, economic reconstruction, the establishment of mixed economies ('market systems with extensive state involvement', ibid: 9), and the establishment of the Bretton Woods agreement of 1944 were all to regulate and stabilise the wilder fluctuations of international and local capital (Sakwa and Stevens 2000). The European region has been able to maintain its position as 'the pre-eminent exporter of cultural values, pollution, economic goods, political institutions, and military conflict' (Sakwa and Stevens 2000:184), and as such today it comprises one of the world's high income economies; a centre of capital concentration and accumulation which is able to speak with comparable centres such as those found in the USA and Japan.

The post war pact in Western Europe tied capital and labour into relations of dependency and mutual containment, and the era saw the gradual reformation of Western European party systems away from a system based upon severe ideological division along an axis which stretched from Communist Left to Fascist Right towards a narrower range, where movements of the outlying poles were discredited, and pressure towards the centre-right developed[1] (Calvocoressi 1997; Wilde 1994; von Beyme 1985).

Thus, the first wave of Boomers in Europe and America grew up during a period of economic and social restraint followed by relative stability and the development of some affluence. The start to the long economic boom at the cultural level was characterised by ideological attempts or 'policies' of normalisation, based on idealised family life and a construction of youth as unsullied by the trauma of the War. However, the strictures of mannered and civilised society, and the widespread construction of what a decent and law abiding citizen might be was to fan the flames of an increasingly resentful youth. Initial youth rebellions were small scale at the level of gangs, but a popular culture fanned the concept of youth as somehow new, with a different kind of life. Meanwhile, an increasingly politicised Black society asked serious questions as to the continuation of policies of segregation and subordination, not least given their contribution to the victory against fascism (Turner 2002).

The economic miracle variously referred to as the thirty glorious years (France), the miracle years (Italy) and the economic miracle (Germany) was characterised in the United Kingdom as a period of unprecedented wealth creation and distribution. The economic pattern was rather less continuous than experienced elsewhere in Europe, developing as a stop-start model (Edye and Lintner 1996). Thus, the post war boom in European states was largely underpinned by the specific 'regimes of

---

1   The fascist and extreme right wing having been delegitimised by the Second World War, and the communist wings being made subject to a vigorous campaign waged by both the right and liberal centre within Europe, and the USA.

accumulation, and modes of regulation that, although different in detail, follow the same broad lines' (Edye and Lintner 1996:119).

The Consequences for the First Wave Boomers

The consequences for the generations were significant. Easterlin (1961) for example locates the parental generation of the Sixties as the generation of the 1916–25 cohort, with a history of war, scarcity and trauma and carrying a dominant ideational direction which was pro-family and national duty. The first wave of the Boomer's parental generation were the children of what I have termed in Chapter 5 the first People's Generation of the Great War, and carried this through to the Great Depression as Glen Elder's (1974) study *Children of the Great Depression: Social Change in Life Experience* shows. Thus, the childhood and youthful experience of the first wave boomers were in marked contrast to that of the parental generation. Elder's conceptual and historical map locates two generations in relation to the Great Depression. The two generations 'are off-spring of contrasting childhoods, one marked by scarcity, and the other by affluence' (1974:5). The parental generation's experience was of '… despair and helplessness, illness and alcoholism; and to mothers emotional distress, humiliation, and a heavy family burden (1974:273). The loss of economic status at the level of family and household produced adaptive responses, for example, Elder suggest that the older generation developed a psychic framework around 'self-sacrifice and earned success' (1974:295). Elder cites Gan's (1967) concept of their enjoying a low threshold of excitement. Elder sees that the psychosocial impact of the experience of the Depression has received '… minimal attention, yet an extraordinary work commitment, a self-conscious desire for security, an inability to partake of pleasure or leisure without guilt feelings' (ibid: 277) was the lasting legacy against which the next generation was to rebel.

This rebelling youthful generation were by contrast '… a uniquely indulged generation … A life beyond the dreams of avarice seemed to have become accessible to those whom fortunes of birth – in time and status- had favoured' (Shils 1964:44). Gans (1967) interpreted the inter-generational relationship as one of parental protectionism, combined with a wish to return to 'normality' and a 'quiet' life. This means that the younger generations were 'protected' from stress and excitement, and shielded from certain kinds of knowledge, such as that of economic crisis. This was experienced by the baby boom generation in the post war era as conformist and even claustrophobic.

Braungart (1984) explored the internal life of four generations (the Young Europe, Post-Victorian, Great Depression, and the 1960s), and identifies the variable of success at effective mobilisation as being the generational units capacity to acquire sponsorship from elsewhere in the generational structure, for example, their neighbouring generation. This is in contrast to the view of action as a spontaneous emergence driven by its own velocity rather than being pulled along and into the intergenerational structure, and highlights the importance of the diversity of interpretations of the Sixties spectacular mobilisations, since different generational units are located differently within the social location, and will connect differently to fore-running generational units.

Laufer and Bengston (1974) also take inter-generational relations as one of the variables, noting that the post war reconstruction and boom '... has had its most dramatic and destabilising effect on the middle and lower classes (ibid: 189). The ghettoisation of poverty meant that movements driving for Black Power and civil rights '... exerted pressure to submerge generational issues in favour of class and radical (ethnic) issues' (ibid: 191). As Elder (1974) also observed, the bureaucratisation of the middle class and its different location in the power had different implications for the children of the Great Depression and the Second World War and the succeeding age cohorts.

The First Wave Boomers: Understanding its Generationalism

The consequences of the inter-generational dynamic and the social situation encountered by the youthful generation of the first Boomers included political ones. These were a change in political direction between the two generations since '... a deep seated faith in centralised government, based on democratic principles, as a vehicle for social, racial and economic reforms' (Elder 1974) held by the parental generation were the target of rebellion by the New Left and the new social movements (Wilde 1994).

The literature suggests that the regimes of Europe had fully embraced the industrial model, largely taking the population with them, in structures of managed consensus and conflict (Crouch 2000). Dissidence in the form of protest which was post-material in character, resting on quality of life, rights, expression and identity was married with anti-war protests and demands for liberation. This produced a new prototype category (Rosch and Lloyd 1978) of protest, the so-called 'new social movements' of the Sixties and Seventies (Wilde 1994), a genre which makes demands of both a material and subjective kind accompanied by what McKay (1996) was later to call senseless acts of beauty.

The social situation and struggle over segregation and Civil Rights in the South of the USA (Turner 2002) and the contexts of the struggle for hegemony in the Cold War which had been unleashed (Wilde 1994), fuelled the dissent of the first Boomers, while the long years of the economic boom and the enhanced vehicles of post-compulsory education and better health care underpinned their mobility. The social situation provided an opportunity structure for the Boomers, who otherwise lacked what the epic generations had experienced at the level of an opportunity structure which leant itself to a discourse of history making and tragedy on the one hand, and social puzzles and role displacement which brought young people together in their search for adaptive strategies, on the other.

I think we can understand the significance of key events (such as Vietnam), and processes (for example the expansion of higher education with a model of leaving home to live on a campus university), as key to influencing the social situation such that generational units could assemble around and through them; gain velocity and actualisation; and act upon the situation encountered. The particular kinds of action were those of an affluent and changing, consumption orientated society. For example, action included the arts and theatre and the use of new media, as well as more traditional street protest. The opportunity structure is not just external to the generation, but can be brought in, worked on and produced at a social level through generational activity itself. Thus, the first wave of Boomers both contributed to and drove new media as well as using it to gain velocity. This suggests a reiterative process between agency and structure which can be seen in generationalism to work in novel and interesting ways.

Edmunds and Turner (2002a) suggest that the changing political and social climate was a direct outcome of generational change, which they characterise as driven by inter-generational conflict. The mobilisation of the civil rights movements in the USA in particular, and of new social movements in Europe and America more generally, developed an opportunity structure sufficient to generate oppositional subjectivities and a move to actualisation (ibid). Edmunds and Turner argue that post material values and counter-cultural action challenged the hegemony of the industrial-military quality of capitalism, while feminist and peace movements challenged its nuclear and patriarchal quality (ibid). This also points to a more reflexive and aesetheticised culture expressed by the outpourings of the generation in its wealth and form of media in everything from film to journalism and comics, to new forms of music, experimentation with the theatre, novels, innovations in social life and love, and new family and household relationships.

Some theorists have read the two generations as expressing continuity rather than a radical break. Mauss (1971) for example argues that the New Left of the Sixties showed a much greater continuation of values promoted by an older Left generation but requiring adaptations to the Cold War. More decisively, Altbach and Peterson (1971) understand radical student behaviour to be a continuation of family and social traditions but in a context where institutions played a particular role, for example, the university structure provided an alternative space which shaped different sorts of political expression, in particular non-bureaucratised strategies.

Picking up on a theme of the generation of Great War explored in Chapter 5, we can see that the change in media (in form, accessibility and popularity), meant that the Boomers were no longer dependent on written words in order to develop culture.

There is one aspect of culture which did blossom – reflexivity and the insertion of the personal and person into the process. One form of expression was the rise of autobiography, including not just those written from the subject position of I/me, but also those of We/us). Hazlett (1998) for example, discusses the production of a large number of autobiographies which he claims can be understood as generational autobiographies. This he explains by suggesting that an 'Individual's private existence is given significance through participation in collective "historical acts"' (ibid: 9) and a certain 'witnessing pleasure' taken in what I would call 'I was there-ism' as discussed in Chapter 5. Hazlett argues that generational autobiographies produced from the Sixties are a particular form of cultural text which can be grouped into Annunciatory Narratives; Reactive Narratives; and Elegiac Narratives according to when they are written after the generational moment.

Annunciatory Narratives are texts which announce the presence of the generation and are laced with denouements and the import of the historical moment which has been identified. Examples include the Port Huron statement (which can be found in the Appendix of James Miller's (1987) *Democracy's in the Streets: From Port Huron to the Siege of Chicago*), the opening lines of the original draft read:

Introduction: Agenda for a Generation

Every generation inherits from the past a set of problems – personal and social – and a dominant set of insights and perspectives by which the problems are to be understood and, hopefully, managed. The critical feature of this generation's inheritance is that the problems are so serious as to actually threaten civilization, while the conventional perspectives are of dubious worth. Horrors are regarded as commonplace; we take universal strife in stride; we treat newness with a normalcy that suggests a deliberate flight from reality.

(http://www.sds-1960s.org/PortHuronStatement-draft.htm
Students for a Democractice Society [SDS] [2010])

While the opening lines of the final version read:

INTRODUCTION: AGENDA FOR A GENERATION

We are people of this generation, bred in at least modest comfort, housed now in universities, looking uncomfortably to the world we inherit.

When we were kids the United States was the wealthiest and strongest country in the world: the only one with the atom bomb, the least scarred by modern war, an initiator of the United Nations that we thought would distribute Western influence throughout the world. Freedom and equality for each individual, government of, by, and for the people – these American values we found good, principles by which we could live as men. Many of us began maturing in complacency.

As we grew, however, our comfort was penetrated by events too troubling to dismiss. First, the permeating and victimizing fact of human degradation, symbolized by the Southern struggle against racial bigotry, compelled most of us from silence to activism. Second, the enclosing fact of the Cold War, symbolized by the presence of the Bomb, brought awareness that we ourselves, and our friends, and millions of abstract "others" we knew more directly because of our common peril, might die at any time. We might deliberately ignore, or avoid, or fail to feel all other human problems, but not these two, for these were too immediate and crushing in their impact, too challenging in the demand that we as individuals take the responsibility for encounter and resolution.

(http://www.sds-1960s.org/PortHuronStatement-draft.htm [2010])

Reactive Narratives, on the other hand, tend to arise in the next phase, which according to Hazlett (1998) is a turn towards the decline of generational solidarity, and in some cases may be more like renunciations than confirmations. An example of this is the Dotson Rader (1969) text *I Ain't Marchin' Anymore*. Elegiac Narratives meanwhile are more complex. They address the person and the generation which the actor(s) have become as well as who they once were. These texts, written after the event and sometimes heavily laced with nostalgia, '… employ various death tropes to figure the demise of their former sixties selves' (ibid: 152). In some cases, they struggle with their historical role and feel the need to claim the authenticity of their experience, not least in the face of its reinvention by social forces and institutional systems far beyond its control. Such a text is David Harris' (1982) autobiography *Dreams Die Hard*, written from the standpoint of one of the former 'leaders' of the SDS who had married Joan Baez, a quotation from which given by Hazlett reads:

> It is hard for me to describe us and what we were about that summer without lapsing into what now sounds trite … we weren't a parody, whatever has since become of our words. We were the "real thing". (Harris 142, in Hazlett 1998:155)

Much of the generationalism of the Sixties can be explained by social change. Long before the end of history was claimed via the collapse of the ideological axis (Fukuyama 1989), a technological transformation which would bring about an informational economic base and post material cultures to some extent disembedded from class relations had been predicted with some curiously prescient accuracy (Bell 1976). The more sombre worlds of Habermas and Marcuse had already pointed up the nature of the brave new (life) worlds as colonised by capital, the population subject to the internalisation of false needs created by a new age of mediatised and communicative sophistication and practiced by an ever more rapacious model of capitalism (Wilde 1994). Murdock and McCron locate and explain the rise of post-war youth culture (which was to have such impact on our contemporary understanding of the generation concept), in the failure of existing youth provision, looking instead to the market and the relations of consumption, rather than production, for the source of youth identity: 'Where the boys' clubs and the Scouts had failed, the Beatles and Mary Quant appeared to be succeeding' (Murdock and McCron ibid: 197). This provides opportunities for generational units with different kinds of identities and habitus to develop. Laufer and Bengston (1974) identified four categories of generational units which came out of the Boomers, characterised as:

Radicalism   At the centre of which is anti-capitalist sentiment and the meaning of quality of life (for example expressed in the 1960s through the Vietnam War, the draft, the civil rights movement and quality of life issues so on).

Freakism or bohemianism   An individualistic cultural rebellion '... which emphasised the need for the individual expansion of consciousness by "getting it together" and "freeing the self" as a form of liberation'.

Communalism   Aimed at changing or transformational action of structures, for example families, labour market, interpersonal etc., and characterised by pro-communal values, for example, rejecting individually based competition.

Revivalism   This is about transformation through faith based belief or paradigm shift, and Laufer and Bengston identify this as focused '... on the decadence of American society', and in sociological terms is explicable through the opportunity structure of revivalist movements for 'meaning and order in an authoritative context' (1974:199).

Thus, we can see diversity within and among the Boomers, and much fot he literature, films and archive materials from that time display considerable animosity between particular sections of the generation. This appears to lend strength to Mannheim's concept of generation, with the first wave of the Boomers exhibiting at least some of the characteristics set out by Mannheim.

The Silent Revolution: Period Effect or Generational Protest?

A combination of affluence, protest and deep social change ushered in and expressed an era of a shift in values, political orientations and social mores towards a less authoritarian, subjective and informal style of political and social life at a cultural level, which Inglehart (1977) argued amounted to 'the silent revolution'. Subsequent research has tended to find evidence that this process has continued (see Inglehart 1990; Wilkinson 1994). There appears to be both a generational effect as well as period effect in this social trend, making it harder to claim that this was all the outcome of 'generational activity', even though we might understand how it seemed to be like that to people at the time. Even so, we can say that the first wave of the Boomers were to blossom into a particular expression of generationalism, and were the first of the major consumption generations which were to characterise the second half of the twentieth century.

Conclusion

The first wave of the Boomers grew up through the boom years of postwar European and American expansion, in the contexts of the Cold War and colonial and postcolonial struggles. It was a time of intense social and cultural change, in part produced by the generation, alongside significant economic growth and diversification of class and other systems of inequality. Significant sections of the first wave of the Boomers mobilised effectively achieving velocity which both ensured their entry into the system and identity locations which allowed them to exploit the opportunities of the time, for example in the media and service sector. To some extent we can understand this as a manifestation of the lateral, cohort type of generational formation in Mannheim's sense. An interesting feature of the first wave Boomers in particular is the intergenerational conflict with which they were characterised both at the time, and to some extent subsequently. This was both at a generalised, societal level of 'the older generation' qua establishment, and locally at the level of family, household and community. This latter feature suggests that the intergenerational system of the two axes of A–B and C–D (as discussed in the Introduction) can split apart and become mobilised in strategic opposition. They reiterative character provides for specific processes of opposition and challenge. An example here is the gender dimension to the Boomer's experience. The mobilisation of the lateral cohort was originally of verbal and visible sectors of the generation (particularly based in educated and middle class generational units) but in due course became split on gender lines. This splitting and affiliation of women raises interesting questions about the relationship to the diachronic familial axis. Second wave feminism is often constructed as 'generational', but using two axes allows us to ask in what sense, and role of both axes in both generating actors to step forwards into the arena, and in providing a bulwark of resistance to change.

In contrast to the tragic and state orientated generations of the first half of the twentieth century the Boomers were built through a different set of social relations and that we can make sociological sense of this phenomenon by terming them consumption generations. The following chapter considers what happened next, within the Boomers, as the second youthful wave hit the market and state under circumstances which by this point had begun to change: the long economic boom waned; restructuring and neo-liberalism rose, and the Cold War ended.

Chapter 6
The Boomers: The Second Wave

In this chapter we turn to consider the second wave of the Boomers, unlike the epic generations they too lacked any significant historical task, and unlike the first wave, were largely unable to develop one, since the groundwork of social and cultural change had already been set in train. Fresh contacts arose for some (largely but not exclusively working class as well as middle class) second wave Boomers by virtue of the restructuring of labour markets and anti-consumption sentiment which developed. The youthful moment of the second wave encounter with the social situation brought voluntary assignment to social spaces shared by others with whom common cause was soon identified. These were around the problems of navigating the dying industrial model on the one hand, and the opportunity structure afforded by a blossoming pop culture, postmodern identity politics and significant gender change, on the other (see Burnett 2005). The second wave of the Boomers never achieved the velocity (or actualisation), or stability of identity on a par with the first wave. Pop cultures, style and identity were ephemeral and generationalism was relatively weak. This raises important sociological questions over the circumstances under which generations can gain speed and force and the effectiveness of adaptive strategies developed to navigate its social encounter with a problematical present.

The Second Wave Boomers: The Encounter with the Historical Stream

The globalised chain of interdependencies on which the long postwar boom in Europe relied became ever more problematical so that by the Seventies, dependency on oil, the drain of the Vietnam war, and the end of Bretton Woods had removed some of the earlier certainties of the industrial model (Crouch 2000; Sakwa and Stevens 2000). This has been argued to have brought in its wake the shift towards flexible production and post-fordism (Gilbert et al. 1992). The growth of the service class and the expanded educational system disorganised social production (Lash and Urry 1987). The social situation which the second wave of Boomers encountered was one of a de-industrialising, disorganised characterised by a neo-liberalism and the decline in the post-war consensus. Adulthood for the Boomers was to be carved out under the changing conditions of a globalising, and in the terms of Giddens, Bauman, and Beck, a detraditionalising, liquefying, risk society.

Lash and Urry's (1987) discussion of the diversity of patterns of capitalism in Europe shows that the key variables which will enhance or subtract from the capacity of a national model to withstand or make use of re-organisation, include; the timing and pattern of its original industrialising impulse; its method of formation (e.g., whether by revolution or other means), which impacts the course of institutional life; and the size and complexity of the economy (for example, small countries with few sectors might more effectively channel resources into them). Under this rubric, Britain was prone to disorganisation earlier than its European neighbours, such as West Germany for example, which better withstood the global shift of capitalism until reunification after which it was more exposed. This transformation occurred at different rates and speeds around Europe and America, and had different consequences for other regions which had meanwhile, become increasingly influential in their own right and had commenced a period of rapid economic growth.

The Boomers thus rose to middle age on the back of thirty years of economic growth, postcolonial relations, the death throes of the Cold War and globalisation. With more surviving birth and childhood and better fed and educated than their parents they went through the restructuring of the post war world, passing their childhood in the Fordist post war consensus and encountering their youthful moment during the time of its unravelling. A case study of this is provided by the UK, where the shorthand name of the period: 'Thatcherism' defines their youthful moment.

Thatcherism and Deregulation

The term Thatcherism was first used in January 1979 edition of *Marxism Today* and was later used in a *Times* newspaper leader (Gamble 1998), yet defies any single definition either by commentators or the Thatcherites themselves (Lawson 1992). It has been defined in part by its economic policy, which was the replacement of Keynesian approaches by monetary policy linking the quantity of money with prices and inflation (McLennan, Held and Hall 1984). The new economic paradigm assumed that while the demand for money was stable, supply fluctuates as a result of changing levels of demand by the state. Surplus demand generated by public sector borrowing caused disequilibrium in markets leading to inflation, the main check of which was unemployment.

It has been argued that Thatcherism was a rag-bag of neo-liberal and contradictory ideas such as the demand for freedom (of some kinds), hand in hand with an increased control and authoritarianism (Hall and Jacques 1983). Gamble (1998) argues that Thatcherism has no unified meanings, and rather refers to a style of leadership as much as doctrines and programmes. This style has been described as pragmatic which enabled a curious mixture of intense radicalism on the one hand, and vision-less *ad hoc* adjustments in the journey of central government and the elite at that time (Ranelagh 1991). The former Chancellor of the Exchequer Nigel Lawson in his memoirs recalls his own definition of Thatcherism in a speech in 1981, where he described a free market approach to government characterised by a firm control on public expenditure, mixed with populism, Victorian values, nationalism and tax cuts, to which his own personal contribution was to have added American style enterprise culture (Lawson 1992). The main components of Thatcherism can be characterised thus:

Deregulation of markets and transfers of property   The sale of council housing; property development and home ownership; the flotations of shares of nationalised industries; and increasingly deregulated financial markets with a diversification of financial instruments, can be read as representing a general desire, policy and practice to transfer wealth from public to private ownership, in what was presented as a wider democratisation of property and share ownership. For example, Kenneth Baker's speech in the House of Commons: 'Home ownership and the Right To Buy represent a major transfer of wealth from the municipal landlord to individual families' (Hansard 38, col. 941).

The transitions in the UK housing markets were to have a major impact on the Boomer generations, both first and second wave. The first wave bought extensively thus pushing prices up and establishing a strong post war norm towards home ownership as aspiration. The second wave had a staggered start in the housing market (as well as the labour markets) experiencing rising house values; relatively high rents; and negative equity: but the crowd and class reproduction behaviour of the UK Boomers across both waves significantly drove the housing markets in the UK for 20 years. Today, we see some of the consequences with the fall out from the credit crunch, as well as gaining an insight into the peculiarly UK (and US influenced) path through the European model, with the cultural preference for home ownership (linked to the British class system) as one of the major drivers of the now middle aged and retiring Boomers making their way through contemporary adulthood.

The struggle for the inner city   Today, the discourse of the inner city has shifted somewhat towards urban regeneration, cosmopolitanism and service centres. But at its heyday, the discourse of inner city (and the inner city youth who lived there) was a powerful vehicle for approaches designed to deal with problems and opportunities which have roots in the interplay between capital, labour, migration, poverty, and the new opportunities which city life afforded such as consumption, and cultural activities as well as of social organisation and political movements (as understood by Castells 1977, and by the Birmingham Centre for Contemporary Cultural Studies, CCCS). The decline in the industrial model produced a new kind of declining city, socially constructed as the repository of the working class, the poor, the single parent, the immigrant etc., the locus of crime and disadvantage.

The rediscovery of poverty in the Sixties (Abel-Smith 1965), provides a context for the emergence of social programmes, (for example the Urban Programme in Britian in 1968), based on a theory of 'multiple deprivation' and from there fanning out to consider where the answers might lie. Thus the Archbishop of Canterbury's Report *Faith in the City* (1985) concluded that the solution to the inner city was a collectivist one where 'the local council is essentially the saviour of the city' (Hansard 88, col. 939). Such sentiments simply fanned the flames of an increasingly savage central-local power struggle (Batley and Stoker 1991) in the United Kingdom (although not so much everywhere in Europe), as the inner city became one of the key arenas through which the battles of ownership and control were fought.

The era of enterprise   Of equal importance was the discourse of enterprise, which came to be applied to, and through, all manner of projects including contracting out; the deregulation of key markets such as housing and financial services; policy initiatives designed to nurture a small- and medium-sized enterprise economy (such as small business advisers; enterprise zones; enterprise allowances to new entrepreneurs; services and grant aid and so on); the highly valued lone entrepreneur.

However Thatcherism is conceptualised, we can say that it was articulated during, and partly contributed to, a period of social and political disorganisation in the sociological sense in which Lash and Urry (1987) mean. Some of the key power struggles of the generation's period of youth and adulthood was to work around the concept of Thatcherism and some of its adaptive strategies were responses to it.

The Second Wave Boomer's Encounter with the Social Situation

The significance of these changes to the youthful cohorts of the second wave of the Boomers lies in the approach suggested by Mannheim with what he sees as their opportunity and ability to make 'fresh contacts' (1952:293). Fresh contacts, i.e. meeting new people, '… always means a changed relationship of distance from the object and a novel approach in assimilating, using, and developing the proffered material' (ibid). Fresh contacts are crucial to the formation of youth cultures, offering peer groups from which generational activity might spring. Nonetheless, the 'fresh contacts' available to the generation as youth included those found in civil society, in the intellectual and social currents of the day. Mannheim places a great emphasis on such participation, stating that:

> Individuals of the same age, they were and are, however, only united as an actual generation in so far as they participate in the characteristic social and intellectual currents of their society and period, and in so far as they have an active or passive experience of the interactions of forces which made up the new situation. (1952:304)

The social situation of the youthful moment encountred by the second wave of the Boomers can be characterised by:

- The continuation of Inglehart's (1977) 'silent revolution' in norms and values;
- Gender change driven in part by the first wave of the Boomers;
- The decline of traditional associational styles of organisations and the general disorganisation of communities including housing classes and occupational communities;
- A general unravelling of institutions such as the practice of 'early' working class marriage;
- Opportunity structures of media, fashion and consumption including practices of youth culture ('being youthful' inherited in part from the first wave of Boomers);
- A transformation in working class life and the rise in diverse identities and communities, such as GLBT, and Black and mixed heritage;
- Thatcherism in the UK; and its variations on a theme across Europe heightened by the end of the Cold War and substantive regime change.

Such social transformations produced both many opportunities for new contacts, (including those which would not have occurred under the organised sociality of Fordist Britain) as well as polarisation and social decline which led to disembedded individuals and communities from the social situation, (partially captured in the concept of social exclusion).

Fresh Contacts: Cultural Encounters

The generation entered an era of fragmented youth cultures, symbolised by many different musical and political currents. The New Wave of the Seventies and Punk had arisen as an outright rejection and critique of the disco and pop music generated by the first wave of the baby boom in hippie and youth cultures. Whereas much of the earlier pop music had been made through a celebrity and 'star' system, New Wave and Punk had rejected these as essentially bourgeois creations (Sabin 1999), and had adopted a nihilistic approach, with a home made, local, suburban ('back bedroom and local pub') model of production, using guitars and drums (Larkin 2003). What emerges from O'Hara's (1999) discussion of the cultures is the extent to which racialised identities were produced through them, for example, white (male) actors flowed into skinhead and Punk Rock, while young black people also had opportunities to become attached to alternatives such as northern soul.

The cultural system however was characterised by continued diversification for example with a resurgence of biker culture, and the innovation of the 'New Romantic' style, which while originally springing from a trendy London base, spread to other parts of Britain as a critique of New Wave itself. Discussions of such cultural movements point to their production within social networks, such as Sabin's (1999) collection of essays exploring Punk and New Romantic cultures as rather than individual 'heroes'. Such developments also drew on previous cultural manifestations, the anarchic and fragmented aesthetic of Punk for example, has been argued to draw on radical twentieth century movements including Dadaism, surrealism, and anarchic concepts (Marcus 2002).

Particular styles of dress and deportment were signals of identification, and as Turner (2002a) explores, can be understood as a form of stylised embodiment which is specific to particular identities and generations. The New Romantics for example, swapped adornment based on cheap, household, domestic and waste products for satin and silk, wigs and clothes reminiscent of fancy dress. Punks 'po-goed' and were prone to 'hanging around' suburban streets, bus stops, and car parks. The New Romantics 'posed' in public places such as squares or outside of a shopping centre, where they could be sure of getting an audience in a distinctively theatrical and self consciously performative mode of self (O'Donnell 2001).

Such youthful subjectivities have been posed as a problem of class relations. Work which considered an earlier phase of post-war youth cultures used a discourse of sub-cultures (see the work of the Centre for Contemporary Cultural Studies, CCCS) Hebdige's analysis of the meaning of such style, in common with much of the CCCS was perhaps rather informed by a fairly determinist class analysis, which for example saw habitus writ large in Punk culture:

> The punk ensembles, for instance, did not so much magically resolve experienced contradictions as represent the experience of contradiction itself in the form of visual puns (bondage, the ripped tee-shirt, etc.). (1979:21)

The CCCS conceptualised youth sub-cultures as a 'double articulation' of working class parent culture and a dominant bourgeois culture, mapped on to a specifically disempowered strategic location of 'youth' (Clarke et al. 1998:15), which then goes on to produce cultural forms of resistance. Such treatments of activism as sub-cultures was later criticised by Redhead (1990) for distinguishing too strongly between sub-cultures and the entire population (since in practice members might shift allegiance quickly or frequently, and the assumption of such a strong division does not accurately trap the variety of means by which participation might occur). It assumes a great importance to those who do participate in particularly active and visible ways. This last point was taken up by Bennett (1999) who questions the internal coherence of such identities which may be little more than gangs, preferring the concept of neo-tribe to capture the loose and networked style of sociality which characterise these social entities. O'Donnell's (2001) point in his discussion is that in fact such cultures have changed over time, and that Bennett and the CCCS were talking about entities operating in different class relations. This I feel to be helpful in locating the generation of this research in its youthful moments, since by seeing youth cultures as occurring within, and made distinctive by, a temporal order, we can see that this generation occurred in a transition point in class relations in Britain. In many ways, such cultures can be seen as a continuation of an earlier development of youth cultures. They have been argued to be the product of post war European affluence, liberalisation and the creation of 'youth' as a modern life phase and a distinctive consumption location.

Table 6.1 The rise and rise of the culture clusters

Name	Leaders	Formation and geographical association	Connections
Duran Duran	Simon Le Bon b.1958; Nick Rhodes b.1962; Roger Taylor b.1960	1978, Birmingham, Walsall, the W. Midlands	Toured with Hazel O'Connor, re-surgence mid-90s
Depeche Mode	Vince Clarke b.1960; Andy Fletcher b.1960; Martin Gore b.1961	Essex: Chingford, Woodford, Southend-on-Sea, Canning Town	Turn to synthesizers and drum machines; Split off to Yazoo
Culture Club	Boy George b.1961; Mikey Craig b.1960; Jon Moss b.1957; Roy Hay b.1961	Hammersmith, Wandsworth, Southend-on-Sea	Bow Wow Wow and McLaren's sponsorship
Jimmy Somerville Bronski Beat (early Eighties) Communards (mid-later Eighties)	Jimmy Somerville b.1961; Steve Bronski, Larry Steinbachek, Richard Coles	London; Glasgow	Burgeoning gay audience and club culture; covers, e.g., Donna Summer; supported David Bowie; Brons
Bananarama	Karen Woodward b.1961; Sarah Dallin b.1961; Siobhan Fahey b.1958	London; Bristol	Sponsored by Sex Pistols drummer; collaborated Fun Boy Three; Stock, Aitken and Waterman
Madness	Suggs b.1961; Mark Bedford b.1961; Miek Barson b.1958; Lee Thompson b.1957; Dan Woodgate b.1960	London and 2-Tone West Midlands	Ska influenced pop; worked through 2-Tone record label
Madonna	Madonna Ciccone b.1958	USA–Europe	New York Disco; Sean Penn; Desperately Seeking Susan
Simply Red	Mick Hucknall b.1960 and others	Various	Collaboration included with Motown records; originally a Punk Rock band member
Billy Bragg	Billy Bragg b.1957	East London	The Bard of Barking, a regular performer at gigs and benefits e.g., Miners Strike

The longevity of the influence and actual existence of such pop cultures was perhaps boosted by the decline in the boom, and the lurch towards the Right wing in Britain and Europe. This cultural environment, as well as economic and social change provided a new opportunity structure which such cultural artists could use, as shown in Table 6.1.

What we can see from such a table is the variety of cultural currents, with their influences in Punk, and the backlash against its largely heterosexualist and macho character, the New Romantics rub shoulders with committed Left wing oppositional characters such as Billy Bragg.

The above table represents a particular cohort which come of age and enter the present in a Mannheimian sense, to find a relatively rich culture and structure which they can work with. The previous machinations of the rest of the boomer population, both in terms of a major pop music industry which had been created, and cultural spaces which provided a rich opportunity structure for the cohort, which springs into the present as the bearer of an alternative culture – alternative that is, to the alternative which has already been put in place.

In sociological terms, there could be argued to be a conformity to the role of youth. Such a view is implicitly present in the Edmunds and Turner (2002a) view of youth generations, as capable of, if not inevitably thrown into, a relationship of conflict as each actualised generation is mobilised through a struggle for entry into the system.

It remains a matter of critical curiosity that the accounts of such youth moments which I have found in the social sciences and cultural studies for example, tends to be fixed upon male actors and a male audience. This includes from within the CCCS, through which for example, McRobbie and Garber (1976) raise the issue of the appropriateness of the conceptual frame of sub-culture to consider women's participation (arguing instead for the concept of 'structured secondariness', which nevertheless positions young women in a subordinate relation to the male actors). However, not all generations are male.

The Second Wave of Boomers: Generationalism

The book *Resistance to Rituals: Youth Subcultures in Post-War Britain* (Hall and Jefferson [1976] 1998) is one of the markers of the changing world of youth and youth cultures which arose with the restructuring of the Seventies and Eighties. The book looked at working class, largely uneducated youth sub-cultures, and many of the themes of the book reflect a substantive shift away from 1960s style of idealist generationalism. Reading youth gangs as resistive through cultural practices, ways of seeing youth, and as youth saw themselves, themselves changed and posed critical challenges to both class and generation theory. As Murdock and McCron [1976] (1998:199) correctly point out in their essay in the book, the youth generations of the Sixties had not abolished class conflict or substantial systems of stratification '… but they had certainly altered many ways in which people experienced and coped with it'.

Youth in the 1970s and 1980s had been relocated in fragmenting class hierarchies and the labour market because of, (in part) generational activity by the earlier Boomers. Age had become one of the critical mediators of the relations of class with the formation of a youth labour market which was expendable under conditions of economic decline and restructuring. In turn, class and other markets of diversity presented a challenge to the concept of generations which had previously presented youth culture as homogeneous. The 'dominant mythology of generations which haunts socialism' (ibid: 207) was up for challenge, and, if nothing else, generations were never going to be quite the same again, given that youth sub-cultures had acquired a new significance: 'They, too, win space for the young', Clarke, Hall, Jefferson, and Roberts (1998). In their youthful encounter with historically specific, dominating class structures youth were once again having different experiences from their parents. As such they developed '… an outlook … a kind of consciousness – specific to age position; a generational consciousness' (ibid: 51).

Bauman's (2000) argument that the nature of this next social phase as essentially liquefying, not least of old solidarities and associational life can best be articulated through concepts such as that of Urry's (2000) mobilities, where it is argued that scapes of the global-local become worked by a series of (not system of), flows. Firstly, such flows are deeply specific, and migration flows are a good example of this, not only to time and place, but to the persons moving. As Fabricant (1998) points out, such flows do not consist of persons of similar status, who have arrived in the flow through similar processes (i.e., economic migrancy is vastly different than asylum seeker, both are different from the world of independent traveller). Moreover, different flows of migrants experience harshly different receptions, echoing Brah (1996) that such flows become constituted through dominant discourses which privilege and subordinate by unequal measure. Secondly, such flows while driving the spatial (dis)organisation of capitalism, also undermine and erode identities and subjectivity tied to earlier social formations, (those of those of Fordist class relations), but do not remove them equally, for all persons, simultaneously, or necessarily with the same consequences.

The significance for actors caught up in these social processes is that such fluidities may in turn create new connections and alternative sites for alliance and identification. The emergence of youth cohorts with particular styles and youthful identities is partly explicable by using Mannheim's experience of youth as a time of 'fresh contacts' and encountering barriers and opportunities in navigating the social situation which existing social scripts cannot successfully address. Thus a shared generational experience and concepts which articulate it, can emerge as similarly located youth understand the specificity of their experience as 'somehow' a sign of the times in which they live, and the issues which they face as special to them.

As with the first wave of Boomers, the opportunity structure available to the second wave included the media and cultural style. The main issues of the second wave of Boomers were more connected to restructuring, deindustrialisation, and the end of the Cold War. The opportunity structure available however also included the activities and consequences of the first wave of Boomers. This is a highly interesting point to consider, since for example, some of the major social changes had included those around gender roles, the division of labour and the transformation of intimacy. The vast majority of the second wave of the generation could not be regarded as tragic or epic and these concepts were not part of the generation's trope. However, some of the major difficulties of youth unemployment, and increased opportunities to women, brought forwards specific social dynamics which were to define the generation's identity. This included the surge of the female sex, including middle class, and educated women of all classes and ethnicities, and some loss of status to White working class men. Some of these dynamics have played out over time as the collective lifecourse unfolded, for example with the rise of the empowered and autonomous thirty-something woman in the Nineties (see Burnett 2005).

Tragedy was experienced by a minority of the generation through the HIV crisis which arose during the generation's youth, while empowered mobilisations of gay, lesbian, bi-sexual and transgendered (GLBT) actors, which had started by the first wave of Boomers were significantly boosted by the entry to social life of the second wave of youth. The Eighties and Nineties saw a major expansion to festivals, music, and organisations of every kind including at the level of businesses and household as well as civil society and in the political world. The economy was boosted by the pink pound rising high, and a significant cultural change to the signifiers of GLBT flowed out.

Black and mixed race communities also saw dual experiences, with the 'discovery' of the persistence of disadvantage and discrimination for all to see in every set of social statistics on the one hand, and gradually improving opportunities for the educated and those able to take advantage of the entrepreneurial opportunities twisting out from government policies and the restructuring economy. Thus, the second wave of Boomers can be constructed as a population which was stratified by a range of specific experiences to produce generational units. Many of these were short lived, moving through transient identity locations with unstable names, and the second wave of the generation as a whole never achieved either the velocity or visibility of the first wave.

In contrast to the first wave of Boomers we can relatively few explorations of this second wave of the generation in sociology as a generation, although there are many studies about youth in the Seventies and Eighties. However, in Becker and van den Broek's (1995) Netherlands' study, this cohort would be part of the Lost Generation, born 1956–1970, who face two issues: a) the 'magnitude' of the previous generation and the economic crisis of 1970s; and b) relative disempowerment, in sharing some similar orientation and aspirations to the Protest

Generation, but lacking the economic and political power to realise them (van den Broek 1995:3).

The problem of social restructuring in the United Kingdom was conceptualised by King (1975) as a time when the containers of state-civil society could be constructed as no longer holding the crises of the times, and thus became overloaded with conflicting demands. Meanwhile, reformulation theorists such as the regulation theorists (Jessop 1988a; 1988b) struggled with the core problematic of how the state operated as part of capital accumulation in conditions of welfare capitalism, and what would happen if it ceased to do so. This moment of the dis-organisation of capital is in contrast to the moment of entry for the first peak of the baby boom, which became mobilised as the Sixties generation. It was characterised by the oil price shocks, rising unemployment, the decline of core industrial sectors and the rise of the service sector. It was also the era of radical and organised feminism, and the female sex born into the second segment of Boomers were to directly benefit from hanging onto the coat-tails of their older sisters as well as both men and women benefiting from thirty years of the march of welfare capitalism and some redistribution of life chances, albeit within confined parameters.

Thus we can say that the experiences of the two waves of the Boomers are rather different, and it is reasonable to expect that the social dynamics which lead to a manifestation of the generation and the forms which it might take, might also differ, outcomes in terms of actual shifts in cultures, norms, and legal infrastructure.

The enduring concept of intergenerational relations as conflict driven and characterised by a generation gap is another. In terms of the career of the concept of generation, the legacy from the 1960s was that the concept of social generation became inherently assumed to be youthful; conflictual; action based; and prone to entering the social moment as a public moment. The second half of the Boomers were seen through this lens during their youth, and thus accounts close to sub-Marxist in style as well as cultural abounded based upon these attributes. But the change which occurred during the social period, and the impact of second wave feminism created in turn different opportunity structures for the later Boomers, who became expressed as a more feminised cohort, professionalised singletons and yummy mummy alike, driving a different kind of revolution shaped in part by their interaction with the demographic transitions on the one hand, and increased educational and labour market opportunities on the other.

These structural factors combined with underlying demographic changes (as discussed in Chapter 4) also generated intense cultural change, not least in the cultural lens of the lifecourse and the understanding not only of the phases of life, but of different experiences between historical cohorts some of whose characteristics rest on the transformation of the lifecourse itself.

Conclusion

The Boomers were a large and complex generation which I have split into two in order to reflect upon their internal diversity. The social situation encountered by both was a social formation which was characterised by significant differences from the first half of the twentieth century. State regimes had become stabilised by the outcomes of the Second World War through the pursuit of stabilisation policies such as the development of welfare capitalism, the development of the European Union, and the events of the Cold War. The first wave of the Boomers grew up through the long economic boom and rode waves of affluence and the opportunity structures of new industries including the media. The Cold War and the vestigial structures of the colonial period and race discrimination generated severe political difficulties, as did the character of the gendered culture. These events and processes provided assembly points and afforded opportunities for fresh contacts and the development of new social knowledge and understanding. The second wave entered this social situation to find that the Fordist model and post war consensus politics were unravelling, while the outcomes from the activities of the first wave in addition were also driving some aspects of social change. The youthful period of the second generation was characterised by a different kind of opportunity structure, an aspect of which was connected with the facing of both the post war period in particular (such as the coming to the end of the Cold War) and the industrial model of global empires on the other. Globalisation, deregulation, and a shift in the political ground unfolded with intense struggles over the relations of class, race, gender and sexuality, and these leant a special flavour to the intellectual and political battles of the second wave. Cultures of style were abundant in the early phase of the second wave, but were ephemeral in both kind and sociological quality. As such they were unable to provide the enduring identity vehicles and fixed labels which the first wave had enjoyed. Generation theory provides explanations for these encounter with the social situation, traditionally in the youthful moment, although more recently throughout the lifecourse, and allows us to look for strategic responses including its attempts to secure positional advantage *vis-à-vis* other generations. A great deal has been written about the Boomers, more than can be done justice to in this short chapter. Exploring the Boomer population in all of its complexity raises more sociological questions than it answers.

Chapter 7
Ageing and the Generations of the Future

Much of this book has explored generations in theory and practice. A running theme has been the association of generations with youth. In this chapter we turn to consider the consequences of a substantial demographic change: We now live in ageing societies. Such societies are characterised by a demographic structure which is moving away from the pyramid (with a large youthful base) to a barrel shape, with a relatively smaller youthful population and a growing senior population. This potentially changes the contexts in which generations not only form, but act. It also means that many of the implicit assumptions which have traditionally informed much generation theory to date, not least their positioning in bottom heavy demographic pyramids.

This chapter begins by exploring the major drivers of change towards an ageing society. The development of a perfectly contracepting society (Ryder and Westoff 1971) which, combined with cultural and gender change is driving reduced family formation which occurs later in the lifecourse (Burnett 2005). The extension of the human lifespan and improved care and pension systems over the recent historical period mean that people are living for longer, and are enjoying relatively healthier periods of older age for longer. The chapter next considers the cultural consequences of large and active ageing populations. It poses the question whether the future of generationalism lies not with the model of the young men of the past but the senior women of the future. The implications of the changing demographic pyramid for society are profound and present challenges to traditional generation theory which rests upon assumptions of intergenerational conflict and the primacy of the youthful moment.

Ageing Futures: The Major Drivers of Change

Changing demographic structures are underpinned by the following major social trends:

- The ageing of populations in the context of lengthening lifespan;
- The decline in fertility.

The effects in terms of generational formation, inter-generational relationship and cultural identification include:

- More than one generation can now be found living through old age;
- Smaller, later and more diverse family formation;
- A trend towards smaller households and geographically extended kinship networks;
- Kith has become important again; friendships, social networking, neighbourhoods or urban identification. Families of choice are flourishing, making surrogate kinship and different inter-generational relationships a reality;
- The caring and exchange practices including financial arrangements are being adapted to changing pension, care needs and longevity, producing challenges to tax systems, welfare capitalism, and finance capital;
- The demographic pyramid becomes barrel shaped, changing the possibilities of inter-generational structure of obligations, dependencies and transfers.

Altogether, we can say that this is tantamount to a third demographic transition. Youth are displaced and the inter-generational structure has and will assume increasingly important consequences for the financial and emotional system of the next emergent phase of capitalism. The first demographic transition occurred through industrialisation and empire building. The population explosion and urbanisation increased the visibility of youth. The second demographic transition was one driven by the female sex and contraception. This heralded the arrival of liberation for women from traditional gender roles and the perfectly contracepting society. The third transition is one driven by ageing and the extension of the human life span, not only in developed countries but as a global force.

The Perfectly Contracepting Society: The Second Demographic Transition

The underlying demographic and socio-cultural trend towards a lower fertility rate was theorised by Lesthaeghe (1995) as the 'second demographic transition' of a similar social significance as the first transition in the eighteenth and nineteenth centuries which saw a decline in morbidity, and a rise in world population growth (1995:58). In part, this second transition is argued to be a function of the Boomer generation and cultural change. The first phase (1955–1970) saw some early shifts in marriage norms with less tolerance of poor relationships and stress leading to a rise in divorce and shorter marriages, combined with more widespread and systematic use of family planning. It also saw significant changes in attitudes, including expectations, towards sexual behaviour and experimentation. Specific statistical blips indicate specific social mores, for example, the rise in marriages due to the social consequences of pregnancy out of wedlock which arose due to the instability of contraception. Lesthaeghe (1995) argues that cultural change between 1970–1985 saw a step change in the decline in marriage; improved and more widespread use of reliable contraception; and cohabitation as a social practice which particularly increased in Europe (although not in the US, Canada or Australia). The age of women at the point of their first child rose to 25 and over. This is a socially significant change in terms of norms and expectations and challenged the arrangements and cultures of inter-generational systems around issues of the control or regulation of sexuality by older generations.

In the third phase (1985 to the present), divorce rates stabilised and serial monogamy became more common, with divorcees either remarrying or cohabiting with new partners. There is also a recuperation effect in birth rates, where the age of first birth moves further into the Thirties and begins to stabilise rather than continue to fall at rates seen earlier. The general underlying social trend is that family formation occurs later in the Twenties and Thirties, not withstanding notable statistical blips including the relatively high incidence of teenage pregnancy in the United Kingdom. The social effects of the third phase have included the rise in lone parent families and the attendant feminisation of poverty, as well as the rise in one person households.

Lesthaeghe used the term the second demographic transition to highlight its distinctive characteristics of its drivers, these being the changing norms and values relating to both reproduction and sexuality on the one hand, and the development of effective, legal, socially acceptable to many communities, cheap, available contraception on the other. The first demographic transition was rooted in the processes of urbanisation and modernisation while '... individual autonomy and female emancipation are more central to the second than to the first' (1995:18). Other views include those found in the work of Aries who traces drivers in the first demographic boom in the increased risk of mortality during infancy and the relatively short life spans of the adult survivors during the years of industrialisation. Thus, having large numbers of relatively healthy children was an economic and social goal in the eighteenth and nineteenth centuries. However, the twentieth century, especially the increased affluence and welfare state of the 1950s and 1960s, saw increased confidence in the survival of children and a changing emphasis towards highly quality investment in children and youth. Widespread social change and opportunity meant that changing cultural lenses framed reproduction increasingly as a choice in the first place. Critically, it was not necessarily part of the logic of engagement in sexually active relationships which could occur outside the context of marriage, for reasons of desire not procreation (Aries 1980).

However, whether the second demographic transition are irreversible or as significant as they may first seem is challenged by those such as Cliquet (1991). These alternative perspectives suggest that first birth has been postponed (until well into the Twenties and Thirties), rather than reduced as such. This argument relies in part on the recuperation effect, both in its scale and its persistence as the new social pattern. Others locate the reasons for social change in other factors, for example Easterlin's (1976) view that the key driver lies primarily in the best size and kind of family unit which serves the economic interests of its inhabitants. Thus, increased wealth creates new inheritance patterns where a smaller number of offspring maximises the continued concentration of wealth through generations while changed labour market conditions, including the loss of the male breadwinner and the gain of the female breadwinner has led to households changing shape. The underlying trend of the survival of the nuclear family not withstanding, there has been a significant shift towards households and family formation becoming feminised, smaller, and characterised by serial monogamy at the head with a diversity of relationships with children.

The Ageing of Populations: The Third Demographic Transition

The underlying social trend of global society is towards an ageing population. Table 7.1 shows the percentage of the population aged over sixty in each region, set against the global average, as forecast by the UN population division. They forecast that by 2050 at least 20 per cent of the world's population will be aged sixty or over, with this proportion reached around year 2020 in the more developed regions. Their forecast also show a continuing inequality regionally, with 'less developed' regions moving closer towards 'developed'. The 'least developed' regions showed some change but not on the same scale. The definition of structural inequalities should be widened it seems, to include the actual fact of lifespan available to the populations in question.

In parallel with this, we see a decline in infant mortality and deaths in middle age. Increased affluence and positive change in other key variables which influence life chances has meant that life expectancy at birth is rising, as can be seen in the case of the United Kingdom in Figure 7.1. The figure shows life expectancy rising throughout the twentieth century with the three major exceptions: the First World War and the aftermath of the Spanish Flu pandemic; the Great Depression at the turn of the 1930s; and the Second World War. We can also see the impact of factors such as welfare state capitalism and better maternity care with the stabilisation of life expectancy since the 1950s.

Table 7.1 Ageing of the world population:
Percentage of population aged over 60

	More developed regions	Less developed regions	Least developed countries	World
1950	11.7%	6.4%	5.4%	8.2%
1975	15.4%	6.2%	5.0%	8.6%
2000	19.4%	7.7%	4.9%	10.0%
2025	28.2%	12.6%	5.9%	15.0%
2050	33.5%	19.3%	9.5%	21.1%

Source: United Nations World Population Ageing: 1950–2050 (Report by the Population Division as a contribution to the 2002 World Assembly on Ageing) United Nations, New York, 2001.

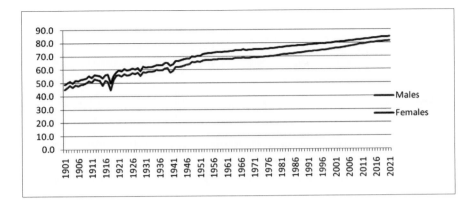

Figure 7.1 Expectation of life* at birth: By sex, UK 1901–2021**
Note: * Expectation of life. The average number of years a new-born baby would survive if he
or she experienced age-specific mortality rates for that time period throughout his or her life;
** 2006-based projections for 2007 to 2021. Top line = Females; Bottom line = Males.
Source: Office for National Statistics.

There are specifically gendered dimensions to ageing, as well as the increased
chances of surviving infancy and youth. Thus, it is not simply that people are living
for longer. The actual shape and gender distribution of the demographic pyramid
(i.e., the distribution of people between different age groups) is also changing
and heightening. Figure 7.2. shows the percentage of the world population by
male and female, distributed across age bands in year 2000. This shows a small
bias in favour of the male sex in childhood and youth which swings towards the
female sex during the later years. Secondly, it shows the relative decline of the
population, this pyramid would show a much greater number of deaths in infancy
and childhood if we looked at one from a century before; a shorter pyramid with
relatively few surviving beyond 70 years old. In 2000, we see the pattern which
has emerged by the late twentieth century, which is a strong youthful base to the
population, with a larger proportion of the population surviving to old age.

Meanwhile, Figure 7.3 shows the forecast for this pyramid in year 2050. This
shows that these trends are forecast to continue. By 2050, the youthful base is still
strong but there is no particular fall-off much before the age of 40. This suggests
a much greater chance of surviving not only infancy and childhood, but early
middle age. Secondly, the falling away which then occurs is still favourable to
a general expectation of increased lifespan. Once past the age of 65 there is an
increased risk of death, but even so, we see that the pyramid has lengthened with
life expectancy for both men and women increasing from 89 years to 99, with a
tiny but important proportion of the female sex surviving 100. Thus, the so-called
demographic pyramid changes in the third demographic transition to become
barrel shaped by 2050.

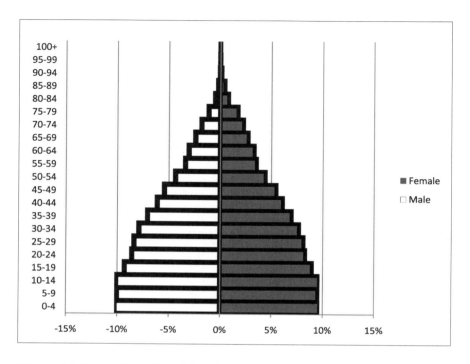

**Figure 7.2 Percentage of world male and female population
         by age bands: 2000**
Source: US Census Bureau, Midyear Population, by Age and Sex for World – Aggregated.

It is easy for readers living in the developed world to overlook the possible significance of many women living this long. Setting aside cultural and ethnocentric lenses, the table shows in effect the dramatic rise in life expectancy forecast in less developed and developing regions. Hidden in the rows of the rational demographic pyramid of year 2050, we see nothing less than a social revolution in generational organisation on a world scale.

Thus ageing populations are the outcome of the falling rate of fertility (i.e., live births to mothers); the increased propensity to survive infancy (i.e., more babies survive birth and early years); and the extension of the human life span (i.e., more people are living longer due to medical advances, technology, and a higher standard of living which mean they are more likely to survive childhood diseases and the trials of adulthood than before).

The period of survival after the age of 60 has lengthened and the quality of life improved. It has become more accepted that old age is itself a period of change, for example, conceptually we can understand the three chronological phases of early, middle and the most aged as well as social differentiation by reason of social stratification. This diversity may spring from a wide range of sources, including:

social class and financial position; generational experience; cultural contexts; as well as by markers such as gender, region and ethnicity.

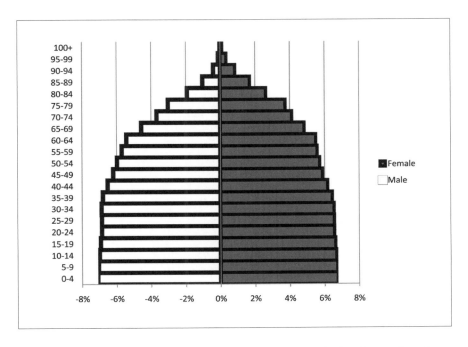

Figure 7.3 Percentage of world male and female population by age bands: Projected to 2050
Source: US Census Bureau, Midyear Population, by Age and Sex for World – Aggregated

The Changing Experience of Reproduction

The second critically important facet of the generational experience is the changing experience of reproduction. Medical and socio-cultural change has led to greater control of fertility and increasingly successful childbirth on the one hand, and changed social norms, expectations and values relating to reproduction on the other. This has led to an overall decline in the fertility rate albeit at different rates and speeds in different cultural and economic contexts. Secondly, there has been a shift in the pattern of child birth within the lifecourse, with the underlying trend being towards a longer period of youth before childbirth. This can be clearly seen, for example, in the Table 7.2 with data relating to the United Kingdom, The modal time for childbirth in 1971, and by some way, was between the ages of 20 and 29. The period under 20 as the fourth most common period, and quite high at 50.6 live births per 1,000 women. By contrast, in 2008 the modal time had moved to now fall between the ages of 25 and 34 years old, and the period of under aged 20 years old had become the fifth most common period occurring in a much smaller incidence than the age group 35 to 39.

Table 7.2 Fertility rates, live births per 1,000 women:
By age of mother at childbirth, England and Wales, 1971–2008

UK	Live births per 1,000 women				
	1971	**1981**	**1991**	**2001**	**2008**
Under 20[1]	50.6	28.1	33.0	28.0	26.2
20–24	152.9	105.3	89.3	69.0	74.3
25–29	153.2	129.1	119.4	91.7	106.2
30–34	77.1	68.6	86.7	88.0	112.3
35–39	32.8	21.3	32.1	41.5	58.4
40 and over[2]	8.7	4.9	5.3	8.8	12.6
All ages[3]	83.5	61.3	63.6	54.7	63.5
*Total births** (thousands)	783.2	634.5	699.2	594.6	708.7

Note: [1] Live births per 1,000 women aged 15 to 19; [2] Live births per 1,000 women aged 40 to 44; [3] Total live births per 1,000 women aged 15 to 44; * Including 'not stated' in Scotland.
Source: Population Trends 137, Autumn 2009, Office for National Statistics, Table 3.1.

In terms of the underlying trend, we see that this direction of travel is not the sole preserve of more developed regions such as Europe. Table 7.3 from the United Nations shows comparative data for fertility rates in different parts of the World. This shows the general decline in births to women. While the data shows that during the 1950s there was a considerable gap between the more developed and all other regions and countries, the second half of the twentieth century sees a growing convergence. Recalling earlier discussions in this chapter of the convergence of relative ageing of populations particularly after 2020, we see that there are common futures for the world's population, within parameters which will become considerably compressed. The changes to the demographic pyramid, namely an ageing population and a feminisation of old age, are global trends, and speak to a conjunction of social and economic change which is bigger than any one cultural change.

The declining birth rate has spurred new thinking about how 'infertility' is viewed and its consequences for gender roles and representations. Remaining childless by choice has now become a global phenomenon yet as has been found by research, voluntary childlessness is still frequently seen through negative cultural filters. The voluntarily childless frequently encounter a reception characterised by disbelief and denigration (see for example Gillespie 2000). This raises issues for those seeking assisted reproduction, partly through the exertion of social pressure which can be two fold. Firstly, the pressure to fulfil the social script of family formation can be experienced as a painful struggle if difficulties are experienced while trying to do so (Letherby 1999).

Table 7.3 Total fertility (children per woman) by region, 1950–55 to 2030–35

	More developed regions	Less developed regions	Least developed countries	World
1950–1955	2.82	6.00	6.62	4.92
1970–1975	2.17	5.18	6.74	4.32
1990–1995	1.67	3.43	5.64	3.08
2010–2015	1.65	2.52	4.08	2.49
2030–2035	1.74	2.20	2.95	2.15

Source: Population Division of the Department of Economic and Social Affairs of the United Nations Secretariat, *World Population Prospects: The 2008 Revision*, http://esa.un.org/unpp, Tuesday, November 24, 2009; 9:08:12 AM.

Secondly, going through the process of assisted reproduction is itself not without challenges. Throsby (2001) looked at the process of decision making needed when repeated cycles of IVF treatments did not succeed. In making sense of the decision to stop trying and its meaning, Throsby found a complex dilemma: was this tantamount to a decision to choose voluntary childlessness, or does it leave the participant(s) as involuntarily childless. Ultimately, the sociological explanation lies in the social hierarchy of meanings in which both the inputs (the methodology: i.e., how) and the multiple possible outputs (voluntary childlessness; involuntary childlessness; conception; miscarriage; still birth; live birth; multiple birth and so on) of reproduction are located. Thus, Franklin (1990) explored the social construction of participants seeking assisted reproduction, sometimes framed by cultural scripts as 'desperate' and victims of childlessness, but on the other hand, the event of live births might be framed by discourses of miracle births or even unnatural births (particularly if the mother was older than the peri or menopausal norms).

Such trends should not be automatically linked to the thesis of the irreversible decline and breakdown in marriage. Marriages are still popular, and divorce rates are more stable than public perception and the media may suggest. A likely explanation for this is in part the rise in cohabitation and the tendency to serial monogamy i.e., the proportion of the population in long term relationships is relatively stable: it is just that they are not necessarily in the long term relationship with the same person with whom they started out.

The relationship between nature, culture and science is a fascinating one to unpick in the area of assisted reproduction, and this and its many cognate and connected systems of research in for example, the human genome project and the possibility and actuality of genetic modification, has raised critical ethical questions which are fundamental to humanity. Their meaning for relatedness, both exclusively human and beyond this stretched to extra-human for all living beings and genetic materials, has produced intense debates and speculations about the nature of life itself from all fields including philosophy, ethics, the arts, the sciences, agriculture, medicine, faith movements and human and animal rights lobbies.

Cultural Change and Equality Challenges

The extension of the human life span has provided raw material to the systems of cultural production which have revised the variety and kinds of lenses through which the lifecourse is viewed. For example, the longeveity of a high proportion of the population in the contexts of economic development has meant that experiencing long periods of healthy, relatively affluent middle age has become much more common. When Shakespeare wrote of the seven ages of man (see Chapter 1) he spoke of all the phases which we today associate with a full timespan, even though life expectancy was much shorter then. The phases were relatively compressed, and youthful family formation took up a greater proportion of time than childhood and ageing at the level of social construction, than subsequently became the norm, with 'childhood' and 'old age' experiencing a long and variable career of invisibility and invention (see Pat Thane's (2000) book *Old Age in English History*, for a fascinating account of the rise and continual reinvention of old age).

The rise of new identity locations and organising principles of contemporary adulthood, includes for example the splitting of the middle age period is itself underway, with the rise of new identity locations such as Thirtysomething (Burnett 2010). The reinvention of middle age is something of a late twentieth century phenomenon, its roots in sociology can be found however. For example, at the level of awareness of ageing, Hepworth and Feathersone (1982) noted that 'Middle age is the time when we first become conscious of the visible signs of the ageing process and the ravages which time has worked (1982:1). The impact on us might well be that '… the fact that others see us as older often comes as an unpleasant surprise' (ibid: 2). The term 'mid-life crisis' arose in Jacques (1965) upon the discovery of the watershed years of 35–39 in the case of 300 creatives (painters, writers etc.), whose creativity either survived or died during this period.

Today and in the future, life spans are such that long middle ages are followed by long old age, to the extent that it has now become the norm to speak of two ages of old age, older and the oldest. Within such categorisations Laufer and Bengston's (1974) presciently observed that the structural conditions which disposed youth to develop generational awareness in the past may be reproduced in old age, in what they termed 'The Prospect of Gerontocratic Generation Units' (1974:199). Since the life expectancy has been increasing, they reason, there is more time to revisit youthful interests on the one hand, and more opportunity for generational units to either re-emerge or to emerge re-constituted in old age. This is particularly likely, given that the driver of generational units '... appears to flow directly from the emergence of a life-cycle period in which self consciousness, choices and redefinitions of self and society are required, or at least pushed to the foreground of consciousness' (1974:200).

Internal diversity to each age set is a perennial opportunity and challenge for sociologists and policy makers. Culturally and in academic discourse, this has affected how we see the lifecourse and understand the demographic revolution through which we are living. An example lies at the knotty intersection of different but connected systems of stratification such as race, class, gender, and age. For example, writing in 1997, '... the older generation in the United States includes more women and fewer minorities than the population at large ... Political debates about age and aging [sic] therefore may be divisive generationally, but also reflect sentiments about race, ethnicity, gender and class' (Mutchler 1997:2). Further, the economic structuring of the population which intersects with all citizens of every age, points up real, material difference in life expectancy as well as diversity in cultural expectations, opportunities and norms. Eric Kingston notes that '... despite the tendency for the entire culture to take on the boomers' current persona as it evolves through the life cycle ...' income inequality within the Boomer population (which he defines in terms which fit only my definition of the first wave of Boomers i.e., those born between 1946–64), is one of the key markers of distinction (http://www.encyclopedia.com/doc/1G2-3402200042.html). It does leave one noting that such major differences substantially mitigates the conceptual usefulness of using the tag of generation, unless we also use the concept of generational units to identify stratification within generational blocks.

Structures of inequality are undoubtedly one of the major problems facing ageing societies. As well as conventional sociological explanations based in demographic variables organised by stratification, Bond, Coleman and Peace (1998) make the interesting observation that old age is no longer a valued status in life, due to the decline in rarity. Modernisation theory suggests that pre-industrial society valued authority and tradition, and thus respected older people. Modernisation brought modern health technology, the opportunity and indeed pressure to retire, the loss of traditional jobs, urbanisation and the widespread adoption of nuclear households.

Perhaps the ultimate form of inequality is that of the experience and circumstances of death. This can be at the subjective level, but for Norbert Elias a key matter was the social condition of old age defined according to the embeddedness of individuals in their social networks (Elias 1985) and the anticipation of death alters relationships and communities. This is also aided by social practices such as the transfer of care of the dying and the management of death to specialist institutions and roles such as nurses and hospitals which however good the standard of care, can disembed the individual from their community (Vincent 2005).

Implications for the Generation Concept and Theories of Generational Change

Since the growth of social gerontology and with it critical perspectives which have challenged the formerly established orthodoxies of 'disengagement' theory and a passive decline to 'sans everything' the human lifecourse at the elder end has acquired a new and greater significance in social theory and disciplines of the human and social sciences. Associations for the study of ageing were established in the wake of the Second World War, including The Gerontological Society of America (GSA) and the British Society for Research on Ageing (BSRA) in 1945 and the International Association of Gerontology (IAG) in 1950 (Bernard and Scharf 2007) which came alongside a substantial growth in the academic area first in the USA and later in the UK and Europe. In the 1950s and 1960s the number of (all kinds of, including biomedical as well as social gerontologically orientated) journals in the area were between 2 to 5, 22 by 1981 and a growth of an additional 23 by the early 1990s (ibid).

The drivers for the emergence of the field of critical gerontology and of the kinds of lines of inquiry which are pursued therein (acknowledging change and development internal to the field) are various. Estes et al. (2009) locate this in part to the wider contexts of the changing lifecourse itself, arguing that the shift from relations of production to relations of consumption influenced the construction of the lifecourse which increased the significance of the phases of the lifecourse which were constructed as connected to production and reproduction (i.e. labour and family). Indeed, the concept of a modern lifecourse, split between sections or segments and experienced in a linear train is symbolic of the production social formation: 'One rolls along in life, just like items on the production line in a manufacturing process' (ibid: 32).

The shift to a social formation expressed and organised in part through consumption, where consumption plays a greater role than previously, affords opportunity for some degree of transformation of the lifecourse. Featherstone and Hepworth (1991) see the lifecourse under conditions of consumption as a playing field. Ageing becomes a 'mask' and the body and the lifecourse become mutable fields which can be re/presented in a series of identities using the tools offered by consumer society (such as trendy clothes and certain youthful lifestyles). The body meanwhile still ages, and Featherstone and Hepworth in a sense, argue that eventually becomes inescapable. The techniques of presenting a youthful identity gradually become less effective, requiring greater and more extreme efforts to manage the presentation of self (for example surgical intervention). This view allows us to see that ageing is both mutable at the level of culture and yet an inevitable feature of the living organism.

This playing field of the lifecourse is promoted of course by the extension of the human lifespan (as set out earlier in this chapter). That extension has opened up new spaces. In practice, for many, retirement (the traditional marker of entry to old age in modern lifecourses lived in the contexts of welfare capitalism) is followed by a period of the 'third age' characterised as relatively healthy and for some sections of the population relatively affluent ageing life time before a much older phase in which health conditions may develop. This third age is characterised as a time of invigoration, activity and fresh engagement (for example by returning to learning, an activity in modern lifecourses largely associated with the young).

The third age can be understood as a function of consumption lifecourses, these being characterised as a decline in Veblen's conspicuous consumption and a rise in consumption as what I would call a mundane practice which expresses connection with modern life and allows individuals and groups to play their lifecourse. This point has been explored by Rees et al. (2008) in their discussion of the historical evolution of the third age suggesting that the term arose from Peter Laslett's work although noting that Thane (2000) indicates that in pre-modern England there was a concept of a 'green' phase to old age, a prelude to decline. Laslett (1996) sees the period not as a function of chronological age but as an expression of agency and collective or crowd behaviour. An aspect of this appears to be an awareness of generational power which is expressed as responsibility for example, expressing the need to protect the environment for future generations. This echoes Eriksen's [1951] (1993) maturity phase which is characterised by a social not just familial recognition and altruism. Thus generational formation and affinity is set out as a distinct possibility in later life, and is not just the preserve of the young. Gilleard and Higgs (2005) see the third age as less taken-for-granted as a quasi-golden age, but one which expresses uncertainty and heterogeneity. In this sense we can say that rather as the years of production and family in the modern lifecourse have changed to reflect a risk society, so risk has now permeated the stages of later life, a process which will be hastened with the decline of pension arrangements and the transformation of finance capitalism which we are not witnessing.

The implications of this at the level of the sociology of knowledge as well as social life are profound. The reconstitution of the lifecourse and generational change are driving new lines of inquiry, the development of disciplinary paraphernalia and grants and trusts. The intersections with the bio-medical industry, housing and leisure markets and the Boomers scale and affluence as a social strata are all driving a surge of cultural interest, if not fascination with ageing while the very real challenges of managing change preoccupy bankers and social policy actors alike.

In the area of social gerontology Bernard and Scharf suggest that a key driver for the development of the academic area was '... the rapid expansion of the Universities from the mid-1960s and the recognition of a need for teaching and courses in the subject' which also created demand for journals (ibid: 143). Likewise,

I suggest that much of the history of the twentieth century including the rise of youth as a social location and the social challenges which this presented, alongside the passage of the Boomers through education and research drove the youth agenda such that today there are literally numerous journals and books, funds, grants and trusts aimed at understanding and 'solving the problem of' young people. Much sociology of generations has been focused upon young people. This is not wrongly so, however what we can expect to see is a rapid broadening out of the field as the Boomers finally hit 'old age' in the magnitude which they represent at the same time as younger women fail to return to the home in the long term. Fiscal crises and market opportunities might accompany both; intergenerational conflict may or may not occur; but the landscape of the generational field will again be challenged and new concepts will emerge to express the adaptive strategies and competitive games of young and old alike.

Conclusion

From the discussion of the second demographic transition, we can see that the site of kinship and reproduction is the object of changing social categorisation and management. The period since industrialisation has seen new shifts and struggles in the terrain by social agents subject to change. The struggle for procreation (outside of marriage, and the fulfilment of women both inside and outside of marriage) and the reformulation of norms governing the nuclear family were the battle ground of the Sixties and Seventies. The 1980s and 1990s saw the rise of the lone parent household and greater sexual autonomy. In turn this provoked fresh struggles in part organised through the formal political structures, the discourses of which locate debates in the resurgence of the right wing (or the rise of a New Right) and neo-liberalism on the one hand, while the fragmentation of social identities with secure social scripts drives informal cultures of working through what is constructed on the ground as social difficulties.

This chapter has explored the drivers of an ageing population, and found them to be in part both the decision making and empowerment of younger women making reproductive choices and the longevity of relatively active older women. This raises important questions over the place of women in generation theory, and the possibility of innovations in generationalism in the future.

These arise in part due to both the extension of the lifecourse itself, which creates the possibility of 'new' spaces such as the Third Age as well as different opportunity structures. These include relations with the market and through consumption the construction of green identities later in life which both mask the ageing process (for some time) and allow different kinds of social interaction to occur based on a playful, active and engaged ageing, as opposed to the model of disengagement and passivity assumed earlier.

Since the demographic trends however show a weighting in favour of ageing women it suggests in addition a new and different context for ageing communities including specific leadership and change possibilities for older women. Laslett's (1996) exploration of the Third Age specifically positioned ageing activity as a collective one, conducted as part of a wider group. This group may well be weighted with a predominance of women for many years, and be split by geographical and regional qualities which will mark out special roles and social locations for black and mixed race women. The possibilities for generational formation and expression in the future are rich and hugely interesting: the past may well have been White, male, young and European but there is nothing to really indicate that this should remain the case.

The move towards the barrel shaped demographic society presents something of a challenge to generation theory and our understandings of the place of generational affinity and identification across the lifecourse. The movement in the axis of the figure on page 2 shows a clear interaction between the A–B and C–D axes. Yet to speculate further would not be within the remit of a sociological text although we can leave this book with a question which only the future will tell. Does the future of generationalism lie not with the model of the young men of the past, but the senior women of the future?

Conclusions

This book has begun to explore the diversity of generational formations by locating them in the historical specificity of the social system with its changing orientation to, and organisation of, time, self and body. Secondly, the concept of generation reflects both this diversity of practice in actuality and the social process of language which allows fluidity over those changing contexts. Explanations for the critique of its usefulness and perhaps to some extent the limited development of bodies of theory and empirical studies of actual generational formations in their authentic complexity (i.e. those which draw connections between and synthesise the formations which lie behind the dual meaning of the concept of generation) are found in the specialisation of lines of inquiry. As we saw in Chapters 2 and 3, these developed as sociology and the social sciences emerged, were consolidated, and became constituted as a field characterised by competition and distinction (Bourdieu 1984; 1993) as well as presenting epistemological problems of scale, size, and perspective which allowed for both individual lifecourse studies and quantitative large scale studies of cohorts to be carried out.

The Axis of Generations

In this exploration of generations I have discussed the instability of the dual meaning of generation and suggested that specific generational manifestations of generation reflect the interaction of, in effect, two related, connected systems of social organisations. These can be arranged along a dual axis of a synchronic, familial or kinship concept, and a diachronic, socio-historical cohort concept. This allows us to see into a system of potentially endless variability and change. Nonetheless, generational formations may express particular kinds of social era so that we may understand a rise and fall in genres of generations.

Antique, Epic and Consumption Generations

In this book, I have begun to explore different genres of generations. I suggested that the discovery of Earth time and of the 'true' ancestors to the humanity in the nineteenth century pushed the escalator of history back, thus bringing forwards and towards each other 'ancient' civilisations of perceived relevance to the Europeans (for example, the Ancient Egyptian, Greek and Roman). These were both sufficiently close to be 'civilised' and sufficiently far away to be 'exotic'. This process occurred during a period when the concept of space was also changing, and in imagination 'shrinking' with a speeding up world while splitting (with a demarcated life span; the separation of night and day time; years with seasons of rituals, and the spaces and places of production and living were moving apart). At least some regions of the world were also becoming more accessible (to rich Europeans) and thus the 'ancient' civilisations could be visited, *in situ* as it were, this act of viewing itself fuelling the concept of people's present and modern, as opposed to those somehow lost or locked in time (and thus not progressive).

These ideological frameworks allowed a renewed interest in origins and a search for the continuity of European history, producing a low level generationalism on the part of the living about the long since deceased, a sort of modern, industrial-colonial ancestor worship complete with special rituals (such as *The Grand Tour* and education in Latin) by which its replication was ensured. I suggested that forms of 'antique' generations were thrown up by this, who stood in contrast to the truly ancient stone age man who was to gradually emerge over the next century. Antique generations are interesting for their connection to legacy, practices of inheritance, and a somewhat 'ornamental' dimension. They are set out to illustrate the history of the Europeans in whichever present they are invoked. They are positioned as 'the same but different' to nineteenth century, modern Europeans.

Epic Generations   The discussion of Epic Generations identified their qualities as modern and tragic, their encounter with history is both their burden and opportunity. Their seriousness of social task and the long deep consequence of its trauma are in contrast to the Consumption Generations which were to follow the Second World War. Altogether more ephemeral in deed and consequence, the Consumption Generations faced the market rather than the state and developed specific *modus operandi* whereby the generation was constitutive of its own opportunity structure.

The 1914–18 generation is notable for the memory work which has both brought it forwards into the present and constructed it in particular ways. Today it still functions as Wohl's (1980) description of being a magnetic field. Its social construction and representation in war memorials, body rituals, literature and special places in actuality are powerful attractors for coevals and subsequent generations, who have both created and hung onto the 1914–18 generation.

I argued that the generation concept was never the same again. It had gone into the Great War in its Victorian clothes of folklore nationalism, kinship lineage, and a thin variety of cohort as social circle. There was in effect a 'high church' understanding of generations, directly related to the 'Begat' passages of the Bible, related to aristocracy and to the class structure, and while disturbed by Darwin and other scientific discoveries had nonetheless been reinforced by them. The Great War changed all that. The generation concept became democratised and was to be applied to working class offspring as well as to the Officer Classes. It was also to become more secular and more grounded in civil society as a place of activity, assembly and identification. To some extent the concept was politicised – certainly its impact on our narration of history was to support the idea that history can be made by people - not only by kings, queens and generals. The Great War in other words, hastened the effect which Marx had earlier achieved, as well as producing new puzzles for the new science of sociology and its cognate disciplines which struggled with the appearance, and loss, of youth.

The Consumption Generations   The Consumption Generations of postwar Europe and the US (although not limited to these regions) were altogether 'different', defined not by a hideous or glorious historical task but rather their positions *vis-à-vis* several entities: firstly older generations, bearing the habits of care, and pecuniary and outmoded social scripts. This produced to some extent an actual social conflict between generations particularly for the first wave of the Boomers. Secondly, the long years of economic boom produced an overall affluence which, while stratified by class and other markers of diversity such as gender in the gendered division of labour and control of resources gained from it, fuelled the markets and led to emergent youth cultures which developed techniques for creating and maintaining identity and positional location.

These consumption generations also carried the capacity for politicisation, the first wave through the Cold War and independence, the second through decolonisation of the industrial model and the industrialised, colonial body. The first wave of the Boomers generated aspects of youth culture which were mimicked by the second, who nonetheless also produced innovations in style. The first wave also produced a fresh mobilisation around gender and sexuality from which the second wave benefited. The two waves of the Boomers are thus connected in a synchronous relationship at the level of power and stratification, as well as in areas of shared symbolic culture and rituals which are apparent when compared to later youth generations (including the 'bookend' buffers of Generation X and Y). However, they also underwent distinctive youthful experiences and in turn were generative of new social knowledge about their condition and action based upon it.

The Generations of the Future   Chapter 7 explored the consequences of the emergence of an ageing society. Much social theory including that of the field of generations has been wrought in a period of the first and to some extent, second demographic transition. This exhibits firstly a fascination and focus upon youth, both as a social condition and a social class which emerged through industrialisation. Secondly, under the second transition, there is a greater engagement with gender and a more synthesised social theory which can accommodate what was hitherto the domestic realm and neighbourhood world of communities, networks and families. The forthcoming third demographic transition however provides us with new opportunities for generational change. Firstly, fresh contacts may arise later in the lifecourse than the hitherto youth-centric lifecourse and generation theory may have assumed. Secondly, the change in the familial-kinship structure is such that mechanisms of caring, reciprocity and exchange are disrupted and will be further so. These include mechanisms at the local level of household and community as well as at macro level of the state (for example through health and pension arrangements).

These changes alone would be significant, but they also drive a further change: the ageing dynamic which is found in many regions of the World and displays signs of convergence over the long, deep passage of time. The youthful generations of the twentieth century felt themselves to be international, yet we have yet to see the consequences of a truly international generation of older citizens. Further, it was noted that much generation theory to date has tended to focus upon the male youth; the dynamics of ageing societies are of female, older citizens. Will we have to rewrite generation theory as a result?

Further Puzzles: Further Lines of Inquiry

I said in the Introduction that this study of generations raises more questions than it answers. As well as Antique, Epic and Consumption Generations, there were other possible formations which may allow rich investigations in the future. These include Silent Generations, and Interim or Buffer Generations.

Silent Generations

Linking the concept of passing and the generation concept is interesting. It seems that one of the accusations of weakness hurled at the generational field occurs when the notion of generation is used to describe activity which is not instantly recognisable as really that of a true generation. This notion, of there being authentic generations for whom the term may be reserved as opposed to failed or non-existent generations raises several issues. The first is that we should be mindful that the styles of generations either attract attention and produce kinds of theorisation appropriate to them or they don't. Thus, one set of issues not picked up in this book, but which surely forms a potential line of inquiry, is why some generations seem to obtain velocity, become visible, and in Mannheim's terms achieve 'actualisation' while others do not. On the other hand, how do generations achieve recognition, and how do the politics of recognition at play in the field influence this? We are left with a first puzzle: in contrast to much of this book which has explored visible generations, how and in what terms may we make sense of silent generations?

Generation theory in all its forms rather assumes that generations do actually exist. Silent generations therefore present a certain kind of puzzle: like so many sleeping beauties lying between the lines of 'really exciting' generations, we find far more instances of quietude than registration. The explanations might vary. One avenue of travel might be that silent generations are squeezed out by their noisy brothers and sisters. This 'quasi-sibling competitive' explanation can be turned into a theory of crowding, which appears in the field from time to time. Alternatively, it might be a cultural problem of recognition. Another set of explanations lie with its opportunity structure, and in a sociological sense we can inquire into the balance of social forces at work and how they may or may not lend themselves as resources and blocks towards a generation. Silent generations are not necessarily impeded by oppressive regimes (including those organised around age sets): a possibility is that for Mannheimian actualisation to occur, a generation must be appropriately bamboozled by the social scripts and puzzles of the day. Mannheim does not explore what happens if there are no particular problems with the social scripts on offer, other than implicitly: a generation, presumably, does not mobilise.

Likewise in its exclusions, Mannheim does not specifically reflect upon or pick up on what I have come to regard as 'imitation' generation behaviour, or 'mimicry'. Mimicry may be an adoption of a generation's (other than one's own) behaviour, or as I shall call it, a *modus operandi*. This refers in part to the generations' style, which can be and is commodified and resold through the market to the next cohort. The easy examples are of youthful cohorts who adopt youthful cultures but this may not be limited to them. Here, it is both feasible and actual that one youthful cohort may adopt the style or operation of a previous cohort in an expression of its own identification and belonging, i.e. in order to make its identity. What are we to do with these? Perhaps this is a form of generationalism with which theories of authentic generations deal. On the other hand, in the genre of the social theory of consumption, we might wonder if the purchase of style and identity renders them the objects of markets rather than the subjects of history. Yet this line of inquiry raises yet more questions: are the generations which are bearers of history more authentic than the generations who are buyers in a market?

Interim or Buffer Generations

Another occasional sighting is of generations which fall between others. These are typically represented as falling after the main event or between two main courses. Yet these *amuse bouche* of the generation field present further questions. They can be characterised as social bookends – sandwiching social mobilisations, they show us both how continuity is created by providing mechanisms which allow 'new traditions' to be successfully inherited (for example by adopting and replicating them) or how they provide the conclusive full-stop to the conversation which has been started. These 'bookends' can bring an end to events it seems as well as ensuring their longevity. Interim or buffer generations are inherently interesting because they raise problems of the loop-like reiteration of social processes and systems.

And Finally

Firstly, we think of ourselves as individual and yet co-exist in a collective universe we conceptualise as society. Thus, we are both an 'I' and a 'We', simultaneously. Secondly, we develop corporeal awareness in infancy and finitude in childhood. In other words, we know that we are born, we live, and we die. This is the case even though the social stream is apparently unending as society flows with a continual replacement largely invisible to the naked eye at a macro and collective level. Thirdly, our co-existence is lived out in the company of a time based cohort of contemporaries in a two-legged race consisting of both a kinship network which structures us in time on a diachronic axis – and an age set network which structures us in time on a synchronic axis (see the figure on page 2).

The Time of Generations

In this book, I have argued that the concept of generation belongs to the cluster of lifecourse, cohort and generation, which address the temporal and historically specific qualities of social life. Cohorts are typically constructed by entities external to themselves, including institutions such as the military and the education system (see Ryder 1965), while generations are unique social formations which Mannheim (1952) argued become actualised through their encounter with the historical present, their development of collective awareness and the development of new knowledge and social scripts which allow them to proceed. Cohorts in contrast are the creatures of researchers. Both concepts struggle through discursive systems of multiple meanings made simple by this book in its claim of a 'dual' meaning only for generation.

Modern generation analysis was claimed by Mannheim (1952) as a problem for sociology. His was a characterisation as a cohort based approach and has a particular interest in the subjective consciousness of the actors and their ability to act upon the social system which they encounter. He describes an intersection between biology and society (Pilcher 1994) in that 'individuals who belong to the same generation, who share the same year of birth, are endowed, to that extent, with a common location in the historical dimension of the social process' (Mannheim 1927/1952:105).

All of this family share a focus on the passage of time and its meaning at the level of structure and agency, as well as individual and collective. The generation concept allows us to discuss the potentially disturbing idea that we are, quite literally, not alone in the universe: in fact, it seems a function of humanity that we carry a dual concept of being both alone as an individual and yet alongside and part of a 'We', a collective flow. The potential explanations for why this should be would lead us to range through the whole of religious belief and philosophy as well as art and engineering. Irrespective of what the 'answer' may be, the problem of our awareness of co-existence over time and coeval relationship in the present means that concepts which explain social and human behaviour must somehow grasp and understand the nature of time and our 'slice' or fold within it.

The study of generations deepens our understandings of lived experience as conducted through communities of time which are both binding and dis/ordering. Generations can be creative and disruptive as well as providing systems of maintenance and replication. For me, the generation concept represents a form of dwelling in time and space. For sociology it allows a move away from the homogenous present to re-imagining the social as dynamic and multiversal in its times.

It suggests that consciousness is stratified between the I/We and Now/Then/ Future. We use this social multiverse to organise our thinking about relatedness at the level of identity, as well as for material systems of obligations, production, consumption and exchange. The generation concept provides for the fact of our co-existence as well as acknowledging its end. It allows for the flow of the social stream which pre-dates and outlives us and the reiterative process by which we make structure and agency in our passage through. In this sense, it holds an enduring appeal to both the lay and expert systems which inform and blind us about our universe of meaning.

Bibliography

Abel-Smith, B. and Townsend, P. 1965. *The Poor and the Poorest: A New Analysis of the Ministry of Labour's Family Expenditure Surveys of 1953–4 and 1960*. Bell: London.

Abramson, P.R. 1974. Generational change in American electoral behaviour. *American Political Science Review*, 68(1), 93–105.

Adam, B. 1990. *Time and Social Theory*. Cambridge: Polity Press.

Adam, B. 1998. *Timescapes of Modernity: The Environment and Invisible Hazards*. London: Routledge.

Adelman, C. 1972. *Generations: A Collage on Youthcult*. Harmondsworth: Penguin.

Agar, M. 1980. *The Professional Stranger*. London: Academic Press.

Aglietta, M. 1979. *A Theory of Capitalist Regulation: The US Experience*. London: New Left Books.

Akhmatova, A. 2006. *Anna Akhmatova: Selected Poems*. London: Penguin Books.

Allatt, P. and Keil, T. 1987. *Women and the Life Cycle*. London: Macmillan.

Allen, N.J. 1985. The category of the person: A reading of Mauss' last essay, in *The Category of the Person: Anthropology, Philosophy, History*, edited by M. Carrithers, S. Collins and S. Lukes. Cambridge: Cambridge University Press, 26–45.

Altbach, P.G. and Peterson, P. 1971. Before Berkeley: Historical perspectives on American student activism. *Annals of the American Academy of Political and Social Science*, 395, 1–14.

Anderson, B. [1983] 1991. *Imagined Communities*. London: Verso.

Andrews, M. 1997. Life review in the context of acute social transition: The case of East Germany. *British Journal of Social Psychology*, 36, 273–290.

Arber, S. and Attias-Donfut, C. 2000. *The Myth of Generational Conflict: The Family and State in Ageing Societies*. London: Routledge.

Archbishop of Canterbury, 1985. *Faith in the City*. Report of the commission on urban priority areas. London: HMSO.

Ardner, E. 1989. *The Voice of Prophecy and Other Essays* (ed. M. Chapman). Oxford: Blackwell.

Aries, P. [1959] 1980. *Centuries of Childhood*. Harmondsworth: Penguin.

Arthur, M. 2004. *Forgotten Voices of the Great War: A History of World War I in the Words of the Men and Women Who Were There*. London: The Lyons Press.

Atkinson, P. and Silverman, D. 1997. Kundera's immortality: The interview society and the invention of self. *Qualitative Inquiry*, 3(3), 304–325.

Badsey, S. 2009. *The British Army in Battle and Its Image 1914–18*. London and New York: Continuum Books.

Baker, K.L., Dalton, R.J. and Hildebrandt, K. 1981. *Germany Transformed: Political Culture and the New Politics*. Cambridge, MA: Harvard University Press.

Balfour, M. 1992. *Germany: The Tides of Power*. London: Routledge.

Barker, P. 2008. *The Regeneration Trilogy: Regeneration; The Eye in the Door; The Ghost Road*. London: Penguin.

Barthes, R. 1973. *Mythologies*. St. Albans: Paladin.

Bartlett, F.C. 1932. *Remembering*. Cambridge: Cambridge University Press.

Batley, R. and Stoker, G. 1991. *Local Government in Europe: Trends and Developments*. Basingstoke: Macmillan.

Bauer, R.A., Inkeles, A. and Kluckhohn, C. 1960. *How The Soviet System Works*. New York: Vintage Books.

Bauman, Z. 2000. *Liquid Modernity*. Cambridge: Polity Press.

Beck, U. 1992. *Risk Society: Towards a New Modernity*. Trans. M. Ritter. London: Sage.

Beck, U. 1994. The reinvention of politics: Towards a theory of reflexive modernisation, in *Reflexive Modernisation: Politics, Tradition and Aesthetics in the Modern Social Order*, edited by U. Beck, A. Giddens, and S. Lash. Cambridge: Polity Press, 1–55.

Becker, G.S. 1981. *A Treatise on the Family*. Cambridge, MA: Harvard University Press.

Becker, H.A. 1982. *Dynamics of Cohort and Generation Research*. Amsterdam: Thesis Publishers.

Becker, H.A. and Hermkens, P.L.J. (eds) 1993. *The Solidarity of Generations*. Amsterdam: Thesis Publishers.

Becker, H.S. 1963. *Outsiders: Studies in the Sociology of Deviance*. New York: Free Press.

Bell, C. 1968. *Middle Class Families*. London: Routledge & Kegan Paul.

Bell, D. 1976. *The Coming of Post-Industrial Society: A Venture in Social Forecasting*. New York: Harper Colophon.

Bellah, R., Madsen, R., Sullivan, W., Swidler, A. and Tipton, S. 1985. *Habits of the Heart: Individualism and Commitment in American Life*. New York: Harper and Row.

Bellamy, E. [1888] 1986. *Looking Backwards from 2000 to 1887*. London: Penguin.

Bengston, V.L., Furlong, M.J. and Laufer, R.S. 1974. Time, aging and the continuity of social structure: Themes and issues in generational analysis. *Journal of Social Issues*, 39(4), 45–74.

Bengston, V.L. and Achenbaum, W. 1993. *The Changing Contract Across Generations*. New York: Aldine de Gruyter.

Bennett, A. 1999. Subcultures or neo-tribes? Rethinking the relationship between youth, style and musical taste. *Sociology*, 33(3), 599–617.

Bergson, H. [1903] 1999. *Matter and Memory*. New York: Zone Books.

Bernard, M. and Scharf, T. 2007. *Critical Perspectives on Ageing Societies*. Bristol: Policy Press.

Bertaux, von, D. (ed.) 1981. *Biography and Society: The Life History Approach in the Social Sciences*. Beverly Hills: Sage Publications.

Beyme, K. 1985. *Political Parties in Western Democracies*. Aldershot: Gower Publishing.

Billington, R., Hockey, J. and Strawbridge, S. 1998. *Exploring Self and Society*. London: Macmillan.

Bonoli, G. 1997. Classifying welfare states: A two-dimension approach. *Journal of Social Policy*, 26(3), 351–372.

Bourdieu, P. 1977. *Outline of a Theory of Practice*. Cambridge: Cambridge University Press.

Bourdieu, P. 1984. *Distinction. A Social Critique of the Judgement of Taste*. London: Routledge.

Bourdieu, P. 1993. *The Field of Cultural Production*. Cambridge: Polity Press.

Bourne, R. 1913. *Youth and Life*. Cambridge, MA: Riverside.

Bradley, H. 1989. *Men's Work, Women's Work: History of the Sex-Typing of Jobs in Britain (Feminist Perspectives)*. Cambridge: Polity Press.

Brah, A. 1996. *Cartographies of Diaspora: Contesting Identities*. London: Routledge.

Brannen, J. and O'Brien, M. 1995. Childhood and the sociological gaze: Paradigms and paradoxes. *Sociology*, 29(4), 729–37.

Braungart, R.G. 1984. Historical generations and generation Units: A global pattern of youth movements. *Journal of Political and Military Sociology*, 12, 113–135.

Brendon, P. 1991. *Thomas Cook: 150 Years of Popular Tourism*. London: Martin Secker and Warburg.

British Library, 2009. Psalm 1, St. Omer Psalter, online gallery http://www.bl.uk/onlinegallery/onlineex/illmanus/yatethommancoll/p/011ytz000000014u00007000.htm.

Brittain, V. 1933. *Testament of Youth*. London: Victor Gollancz.

Brown, M. 2008. *The Wipers Times: The Complete Series of the Famous Wartime Trench Newspaper*. London: Max Press.

Brown, R. and Kulik, J. 1977. Flashbulb memories. *Cognition*, 5(1), 73–99.

Bryant, A. 1987. *Rethinking the Lifecycle*. Basingstoke: Macmillan.

Bryman, A. 2001. *Social Research Methods*. Oxford: Oxford University Press.

Buckingham, D. 2000. *After the Death of Childhood: Growing Up in the Age of Electronic Media*. Cambridge: Polity Press.

Budreau, L.M. 2008. The politics of remembrance: The gold star mothers' pilgrimage and America's fading memory of the Great War. *The Journal of Military History*, 72 (April), 371–411.

Bulmer, M. 1980. Why don't sociologists make more use of official statistics? *Sociology*, 14, 505–523.

Burnett, J. 2003. Let me entertain you: Strategies and issues in researching a thirtysomething generation, in *Sociological Research Online*, November, 8(4), http://www.socresonline.org.uk/8/4/burnett.html.

CACI, 1993. *ACORN User Guide*. London: CACI Information Services.

Calder, B.J. 1977. Focus groups and the nature of qualitative marketing research. *Journal of Marketing Research*, 14, 353–64.

Calvocoressi, P. 1997. *Fall Out: World War II and the Shaping of Postwar Europe*. Harlow: Addison Wesley Longman.

Cherrington, R. 1997. Generational issues in China: A case study of the 1980s generation of young intellectuals. *British Journal of Sociology*, 48(2), 302–320.

Clarke, J., Hall, S., Jefferson, T. and Roberts, B. [1976] 1998. Subcultures, cultures and class, in *Resistance through Rituals: Youth Sub-Cultures in Post-War Britain*, edited by S. Hall and T. Jefferson. London: Routledge, 3–59.

Cliquet, R. 1991. *The Second Demographic Transition: Fact or Fiction?* Strasbourg: Council of Europe.

Coffey, A. and Atkinson, P. 1996. *Making Sense of Qualitative Data: Complementary Research Strategies*. London: Sage.

Coleman, D. and Chandola, T. 1999. Britain's place in Europe's population, in *Changing Britain: Families and Households in the 1990s*, edited by S. McRae. Oxford: Oxford University Press, 37–67.

Collins, R. 1998. *The Sociology of Philosophies: A Global Theory of Intellectual Change*. Cambridge, MA: The Belknap Press of Harvard University Press.

Comte, A. 1869. *Cours de Philosophie Positive*. Brussels: Culture et Civilisation.

Concialdi, P. 2000. Demography, the labour market and competitiveness, in *Pensions in the European Union: Adapting to Economic and Social Change*, edited by G. Hughes and J. Stewart. Norwell, MA: Kluwer Academic Publishers.

Connerton, P. 2003. *How Societies Remember*. Oxford: Oxford University Press.

Connolly, M. 2002. *The Great War: Memory and Ritual Commemoration in the City and East London 1916–1939*. Royal Historical Society New Series. Rochester, New York: Boydell.

Corsten, M. 1999. The time of generations. *Time and Society*, 8(2), 270–272.

Coser, L. 1971. Karl Mannheim 1893–1947, in *Masters of Sociological Thought*. New York: Harcourt Brace Jovanovich, 429–63.

Coupland, D. 1991. *Generation X: Tales of an Accelerated Culture*. New York: St. Martin's Press.

Craig, W.J. (ed.) 1980. *Shakespeare: Complete Works*. Oxford: Oxford University Press.

Crapanzano, V. 1985. *Tuhami: Portrait of a Moroccan*. Chicago: University of Chicago Press.

Crouch, C. 1999. *Social Change in Western Europe*. Oxford: Oxford University Press.

Crowther, B. 1955. The screen delinquency: Rebel without cause has debut at Astor, *New York Times*, 27 October, 28.

Cumming, E. and Henry, W.E. 1961. *Growing Old*. New York: Basic Books.

Deacon, B. 1997. *Global Social Policy: International Organisations and the Future of Welfare*. London: Sage.

Davies, K. 2001. *Women, Time and the Weaving of the Strands of Everyday Life*. Aldershot: Avebury.

Deleuze, G. and Guattari, F. 2002. *A Thousand Plateaus: Capitalism and Schizophrenia*. London and New York: Continuum Books.

Dewilde, C. 2002. The financial consequences of relationship dissolution for women in western Europe, in *The Gender Dimension of Social Change: The Contribution of Dynamic Research to the Study of Women's Life Courses*, edited by E. Ruspini and A. Dale. Bristol: Policy Press, 81–110.

Dominelli, L. 1991. *Women Across Continents: Feminist Comparative Social Policy*. London: Harvester Wheatsheaf.

Dorling, D. and Thomas, B. 2004. *People and Places: A 2001 Census Atlas of the UK*. Bristol: The Policy Press.

Douglas, S. 1995. *Where the Girls Are: Growing Up Female with the Mass Media*. New York: Three Rivers Press.

Dowd, J.J. 1984. Beneficence and the aged. *Journal of Gerontology*, 30, 102–8.

Easterlin, R.A. 1961. The American baby boom in historical perspective. *American Economic Review*, 51, 869–911.

Easterlin, R.A. 1976. The conflict between aspirations and resources. *Population and Development Review*, 2(3/4), 417–425.

Edmunds, J. and Turner, B. 2002a. *Generations, Culture and Society*. Buckingham: Open University.

Edmunds, J. and Turner, B. (eds) 2002b. *Generational Consciousness, Narrative, and Politics*. Oxford: Rowman and Littlefield.

Edye, D. and Lintner, V. 1996. *Contemporary Europe*. Hemel Hempstead: Prentice Hall.

Eisenstadt, S.N. 1956. *From Generation to Generation: Age Groups and Social Structure*. New York: Free Press.

Elder, G.H. 1974. *Children of the Great Depression: Social Change in Life Experience*. Chicago: Chicago University Press.

Elder, G.H. and Pellerin, L.A. 1998. Linking history and human lives, in *Methods of Life Course Research: Qualitative and Quantitative Approaches*, edited by J.Z. Giele and G.H. Elder. London: Sage, 264–294.

Elias, N. 1978. *The Civilizing Process*. Oxford: Blackwell.

Elias, N. 1985. *The Loneliness of the Dying*. Oxford: Blackwell

Erben, M. 1998. *Biography and Education: A Reader*. London: Falmer Press.

Erikson, E. [1951] 1993. *Childhood and Society*. New York: Norton.

Eriksen, T.H. [1995] 2001. *Small Places, Large Issues: An Introduction to Social and Cultural Anthropology*. London: Pluto Press.

Esping-Andersen, G. 1996. *Welfare States in Transition: National Adaptations to Global Strategies*. London: Sage.

Estes, C.L., Biggs, S. and Phillipson, C. 2009. *Social Theory, Social Policy and Ageing: A Critical Introduction*. Maidenhead: Open University Press.

Evans-Pritchard, E.E. 1940. *The Nuer*. Oxford: Clarendon.

Eyerman, R. 2002. Intellectuals and the construction of an African American identity: Outlining a generational approach, in *Generational Consciousness, Narrative, and Politics*, edited by J. Edmunds and B. Turner. Oxford: Rowman and Littlefield.

Eyerman, R. and Turner, B.S. 1998. Outline of a theory of generations. *European Journal of Social Theory*, 1(1), 91–106.

Faugier, J. and Sargeant, M. 1997. Sampling hard to reach populations. *Journal of Advanced Nursing*, 26, 790–97.

Featherstone, M. and Hepworth, M. 1991. The mask of ageing and the postmodern lifecourse, in *The Body, Social Process and Cultural Theory*, edited by M. Featherstone, M. Hepworth, and B.S. Turner. London: Sage, 371–389.

Featherstone, M. and Wernick, A. (eds) 1995. *Images of Aging: Cultural Representations of Later Life*. London: Routledge.

Filakti, H. 1997. Trends in abortion 1990–1995. *Population Trends*, 87, 11–19.

Finch, J. 1989. *Family Obligations and Social Change*. Cambridge: Polity Press.

Folkenflik, R. 1993. *The Culture of Autobiography*. Stanford: Stanford University Press.

Fothergill, R.A. 1974. *The Private Chronicles: A Study of English Diaries*. London: Oxford University Press.

Foucault, M. 1986. Of other spaces: Heterotopias. *Diacritics*, 16, 22–27.

Foucault, M. 2003. *The Birth of the Clinic*. London: Routledge.

Franklin, S. 1990. Deconstructing 'Desperateness': The social construction of infertility in popular representations of new reproductive technologies, in *The New Reproductive Technologies*, edited by M. McNeil, I. Varcoe and S. Yearley. London: Macmillan, 200–229.

French, M. 1992. *The War Against Women*. New York: Summit Books.

Frith, S. 1993. Youth/music/television, in *Sound and Vision: The Music Video Reader*, edited by S. Firth, A. Goodwin and L. Grossberg. London: Routledge, 67–84.

Fussell, P. 2000 [1975]. *The Great War and Modern Memory*. Oxford and New York: Oxford University Press.

Fukuyama, F. 1989. *The End of History*. Washington, DC: Irving Kristol.

Gagnier, R. 1991. *Subjectivities: A History of Self-Representation in Britain, 1832–1920*. Oxford: Oxford University Press.

Gamble, A. 1998. *The Free Economy and the Strong State: The Politics of Thatcherism*. Basingstoke: Macmillan.

Gans, H.J. 1967. *The Levittowners*. New York: Pantheon.

Geertz, C. [1973] 1993. *The Interpretation of Cultures*. London: Fontana.

Gell, A. 1992. *The Anthropology of Time*. Oxford: Berg.

Gerrard, N. 1999. Is this the future of British art? *Life: The Observer Magazine*. 10 January, 12–15.

Giddens, A. 1991. *Modernity and Self-Identity*. Cambridge: Polity Press.

Giddens, A. 1992. *The Transformation of Intimacy: Sexuality, Love and Eroticism in Modern Societies*. Cambridge: Polity Press.

Giddens, A. 1994. Living in a post-traditional society, in *Reflexive Modernisation: Politics, Tradition and Aesthetics in the Modern Social Order*, edited by U. Beck, A. Giddens and S. Lash. Cambridge: Polity Press, 56–109.

Gilbert, N., Burrows, R. and Pollert, A. (eds) 1992. *Fordism and Flexibility: Divisions and Change*. London: Macmillan.

Giele, J.Z. and Holst, E. (eds) 2004. *Changing Life Patterns in Western Industrial Societies*. London: Elsevier.

Gilleard, C. and Higgs, P. 2005. *Contexts of Ageing: Self, Citizen and the Body*. Harlow: Prentice Hall.

Gillespie, R. 2000. When no means no: Disbelief, disregard and deviance as discourses of voluntary childlessness. *Women's Studies International Forum*, 23(2), 223–234.

Glenn, N.D. 1977. *Cohort Analysis*. London: Sage.

Glenn, N.D. and Grimes, M.D. 1968. Aging, voting and political interest. *American Sociological Review*, August, 563–575.

Glick, P. 1947. The family lifecycle. *American Sociological Review*, 12, 164–74.

Goldthorpe, J. (ed.) 1984. *Order and Conflict in Contemporary Capitalism: Studies in the Political Economy of Western European Nations*. Oxford: Clarendon Press.

Gornick, J.C. and Meyers, M.K. 2004. Welfare regimes in relation to paid work and care, in *Changing Life Patterns in Western Industrial Societies*, edited by J.Z. Giele and E. Holst. Netherlands: Elsevier, 45–67.

Gowland, D., O'Neill, B. and Dunphy, R. 2000. *The European Mosaic: Contemporary Politics, Economics and Culture*. Harlow: Longman.

Halbwachs, M. [1925] [1941] 1992. *On Collective Memory*. Chicago: University of Chicago Press.

Hall, P.A., Hayward, J. and Machin, H. 1994. *Developments in French Politics*. London: Macmillan.

Hall, G.S. 1904. *Adolescence: Its Psychology and Its Relations to Physiology, Anthropology, Sociology, Sex, Crime, Religion and Education*. New York: Aleton.

Hall, S., Critcher, C., Jefferson, T., Clarke, J. and Roberts, B. 1979. *Policing the Crisis*. London: Macmillan.

Hall, S. and Jacques, M. 1983. *The Politics of Thatcherism*. London: Lawrence and Wishart.

Hall, S. and Jefferson, T. (eds) 1976. *Resistance through Rituals: Youth Subcultures in Post War Britain*. London: Hutchinson.

Hall, S. and du Gay, P. 2000. *Questions of Cultural Identity*. London: Sage.

Hallam, E. and Hockey, J. 2001. *Death, Memory and Material Culture*. Oxford: Berg.

Hammersley, M. 1989. *The Dilemma of Qualitative Method: Herbert Blumer and the Chicago School*. London: Routledge.

Haraway, D. 1991. *Simians, Cyborgs and Women: The Reinvention of Nature*. New York: Routledge.

Harding, S. 1991. *Whose Science? Whose Knowledge? Thinking from Women's Lives*. Milton Keynes: Open University Press.

Hareven, T.K. 1978. The search for generational memory: Tribal rites in industrial society. *Daedalus*, 107(4), 137–49.

Hareven, T.K. 1982. *Family Time and Industrial Time*. Cambridge: Cambridge University Press.

Hareven, T.K. 2000. *Families, History, and Social Change: Life Course and Cross-Cultural Perspectives*. Oxford: Westview Press.

Harris, D. 1982. *Dreams Die Hard*. New York: St. Martin's Press.

Hastrup, K. 1995. *A Passage to Anthropology: Between Experience and Theory*. London: Routledge.

Hazlett, T.D. 1998. *My Generation: Collective Autobiography and Identity Politics*. Wisconsin: University of Wisconsin.

Hebdige, D. 1979. *Subculture: The Meaning of Style*. London: Methuen.

Heide, M.J. 1995. *Television Culture and Women's Lives: Thirtysomething and the Contradictions of Gender*. Philadelphia: University of Pennsylvania Press.

Helsinger, H.,1971. Images on the beatus page of some medieval manuscripts. *Art Bulletin*, 53, 161–176.

Hepworth, M. and Featherstone, M. 1982. *Surviving Middle Age*. Oxford: Blackwell.

Hesiod, 1999. *Theogony* and *Works and Days* (trans. M.L. West). Oxford: Oxford University Press.

Hockey, J. and James, A. 2003. *Social Identities across the Lifecourse*. Basingstoke: Palgrave Macmillan.

Hockey, J. and James, A. 1993. *Growing Up and Growing Old*. London: Sage.

Hoffman, A. 1968. *Revolution for the Hell of it*. New York: Dial.

Hoffman, A. 1980. *Soon to be a Major Motion Picture*. New York: Putnam's.

Hohn, C. 1987. The family lifecycle: Needed extensions of the concept, in *Family Demography*, edited by J. Bongaarts, T. Burch, and K. Wachter. Oxford: Clarendon Press, 65–80.

Holmes, R. 2005. *Tommy: The British Soldier on the Western Front 1914–18*. London: Harper Perennial.

Hoskings, J. 1998. *Biographical Objects: How Things Tell the Stories of People's Lives*. London: Routledge.

Hughes, G. and Stewart, J. (eds) 2000. *Pensions in the European Union: Adapting to Economic and Social Change*. Boston: Kluwer Academic Publishers.

Ikels, C. et al. 1992. Perceptions of the Adult Life Course: A Cross Cultural Analysis. *Ageing and Society*, 12, 49–84.

Inglehart, R. 1977. *The Silent Revolution: Changing Values and Political Styles Among Western Publics*. Princeton: Princeton University Press.

Inglehart, R. 1990. *Culture Shift in Advanced Industrial Society*. Princeton: Princeton University Press.

Irwin, S. 1996. Age related distributive justice and claims on resources. *British Journal of Sociology*, 47(1), 68–92.

Irwin, S. 1999. *Reproductive Regimes: Gender, Generation and Changing Patterns of Fertility*. University of Leeds: Working Paper 16, Centre for Research on Family, Kinship and Childhood.

Jacques, E. 1965. Death and the mid-life crisis. *International Journal of Psychoanalysis*, 46, 502–514.

Jalland P. 1996. *Death in the Victorian Family*. Oxford: Oxford University Press.

Jessop, B. 1988a. Neo-Conservative regimes and the transition to post-Fordism: The cases of Great Britain and West Germany, in *Capitalist Development and Crisis Theory*, edited by M. Gottdiener and N. Komninos. New York: St. Martin's Press, 261–299.

Jessop, B. 1988b. Regulation theory, post-Fordism and the state: More than a reply to Werner Bonefield. *Capital and Class*, 34, 147–168.

Joll, J. 1990. *Europe Since 1870*. London: Penguin.

Jones, I.R., Hyde, M., Victor, C.R., Wiggins, R.D., Gilleard, C. and Higgs, P. 2008. *Ageing in a Consumer Society: From Passive to Active Consumption in Britain*. Bristol: Policy Press.

Joshi, H. 1990. The changing form of women's economic dependency, in *The Changing Population of Britain*, edited by H. Joshi. Oxford: Basil Blackwell.

Joyce, J. [1914–15] 2000. *A Portrait of the Artist as a Young Man*. London: Penguin Classics.

Kemp, B. 2006. *Ancient Egypt: Anatomy of a Civilisation* (2nd edn, ed.). London: Routledge.

Kern, S. 2000. *The Culture of Time and Space 1880–1918*. Cambridge, MA: Harvard University Press.

Kerr, C. 1983. *The Future of Industrial Societies: Convergence or Continuing Diversity?* Cambridge, MA: Harvard University Press.

Kettler, D., Meja, V. and Stehr, N. 1984. *Karl Mannheim*. London: Tavistock.

Kertzer, D. 1991. Household and gender in a life-course perspective, in *Women, Households and Change*, edited by E. Masini and S. Stratigos. Tokyo: United Nations University Press.

King, A. 1975. Overload: Problems of government in the 1970s. *Political Studies*, 23, 162–96.

Kingston, E. 1992. *The Diversity of the Baby Boom Generation: Implications for Their Retirement Years*. American Association of Retired Persons, http://www.encyclopedia.com/doc/1G2-3402200042.html.

Korff, G., Bendix, J. and Bendix, R. 1999. Reflections on the Museum. *Journal of Folklore Research*, 36(2/3), 267–270.

Koselleck, R. 1985. *Futures Past: The Semantics of Historical Time*. Cambridge: MIT Press.

Ladd, E.C. 1993. The twentysomethings: 'Generation Myths' revisited. *Public Perspectives*, 5, 14–18.

Larkin, C. 2003. *The Virgin Encyclopedia of 80s Music*. London: Virgin Books.

Lash, S. and Urry, J. 1987. *The End of Organized Capitalism*. Cambridge: Polity Press.

Laslett, P. 1996. *A Fresh Map of Life: The Emergence of the Third Age*. Basingstoke: Macmillan.

Laufer, R.S. and Bengston, V.L. 1974. Generations, aging, and social stratification: On the development of generational units. *Journal of Social Issues*, 30(3), 181–205.

Lawson, N. 1992. *The View from No. 11: Memories of a Tory Radical*. London: Bantam.

Leccardi, C. 1996. Rethinking social time: Feminist perspectives. *Time and Society*, 5(2), 353–79.

Le Goff, J. 1992. *History and Memory*. New York: Columbia University.

Lesthaeghe, R. 1995. The second demographic transition in western countries: An interpretation, in *Gender and Family Change in Industrialized Countries*, edited by K.O. Mason and A.M. Jensen. Oxford: Clarendon Press, 17–62.

Letherby, G. 1999. Other than mother and mothers as others: The experience of motherhood and non-motherhood in relation to 'infertility' and 'involuntary childlessness'. *Women's Studies International Forum*, 22(3), 359–372.

Letherby, G. 2003. Battle of the gametes: Cultural representations of 'medically' assisted conception, in *Gender, Identity and Reproduction: Social Perspectives*, edited by S. Earle and G. Letherby. Basingstoke: Macmillan, 50–65.

Lewis, J. 1992. Gender and the development of welfare regimes. *Journal of European Social Policy*, 2(3), 159–173.

Lewis, J. (ed.) 1993. *Women and Social Policies in Europe: Work, Family and the State*. Cheltenham: Elgar.

Lewis, O. 1961. *Children of Sanchez: Autobiography of a Mexican Family*. New York: Random House.

Levinson, D.J., Darrow, C.N., Klein, E.B., Levinson, M.H. and McKee, B.J. 1978. *The Seasons of a Man's Life*. New York: Knopf.

Levi-Strauss, C. 1966 *The Savage Mind*. Chicago: Chicago University Press.

Levi-Strauss, C. 1969. *The Elementary Structures of Kinship*. London: Tavistock.

Levy, M.J. 1952. *The Structure of Society*. Princeton, New York: Princeton University Press.

Longhurst, B. 1989. *Karl Mannheim and the Contemporary Sociology of Knowledge*. Basingstoke: Macmillan.

Lury, C. 1999. *Consumer Culture*. Cambridge: Polity Press.

McCracken, G. 1988. *Culture and Consumption: New Approaches to the Symbolic Character of Consumer Goods and Activities*. Bloomington and Indianapolis: Indiana University Press.

McKay, G. 1996. *Senseless Acts of Beauty: Cultures of Resistance*. London: Verso.

McRobbie, A. and Garber, J. [1976] 1998. Girls and subcultures: An exploration, in *Resistance through Rituals: Youth Subcultures in Post-War Britain*, edited by S. Hall and T. Jefferson. London: Hutchinson, 209–222.

Male, E. 1973. *The Gothic Image: Religious Art in France of the Thirteenth Century*. London: HarperCollins.

Mangen, D.J., Bengston, V.L. and Landry, P.H. (eds) 1988. *The Measurement of Intergenerational Relations*. Beverly Hills: Sage Publications.

Manheim, E. 1947. Karl Mannheim 1893–1947. *The American Journal of Sociology*, 52(6), 471–473.

Mannheim, K. [1927] 1952. Essay on the problem of generations, in K. Mannheim, *Essays on the Sociology of Knowledge*. London: RKP and the remainder of the text.

Mannheim, K. 1936. *Ideology and Utopia*. New York: Harcourt Brace Jovanovich.

Marcus, G. 2002. *Lipstick Traces: A Secret History of the Twentieth Century*. London: Faber and Faber.

Marshall, M.H. 1998. *Making Bits and Pieces Mosaics: Creative Projects for Home and Garden*. North Adams, MA: Storey Publishing.

Marx, K. and Engels F. 1976. *Collected Works*, *Volume 6*. London: Lawrence and Wishart.

Mason, K.O. and Jensen, A.-M. 1995. *Gender and Family Change in Industrialised Countries*. Oxford: Clarendon Press.

Mauss, A.L. 1971. The lost promises of reconciliation: New versus old left. *Journal of Social Issues*, 27, 1–20.

Mauss, M. 1973. Techniques of the Body. *Economy and Society*, 2, 70–88.

Mauss, M. [1924] 1954. *The Gift*. London: Cohen and West.

Mauss, M. 1985. A category of the human mind: The notion of person, the notion of self, in *The Category of the Person: Anthropology, Philosophy, History*, edited by M. Carrithers, S. Collins and S. Lukes. Cambridge: Cambridge University Press, 1–25.

May, J. and Thrift, N. 2001. *Timespace: Geographies of Temporality*. London: Routledge.

Mead, G.H. 1934. *Mind, Self and Society from the Standpoint of a Social Behaviourist*. Chicago: University of Chicago Press.

Mendras, H. and Cole, A. 1988. *Social Change in Modern France*. Cambridge: Cambridge University Press. Originally: *La Seconde Revolution Français*. Paris: Gallimard.

Mentré, F. 1920. *Les Générations Sociales*. Paris.

Mény, Y. 1993. *Government and Politics in Western Europe: Britain, France, Italy, Germany*. Oxford: Oxford University Press.

Meja, V. and Kettler, D. 1993. Introduction, in *From Karl Mannheim*, edited by K.H. Wolff. London: Transaction Publishers, 7–26.

Middleton, D. and Edwards, D. 1990. *Collective Remembering*. London: Sage.

Miller, J. 1987. *Democracy is in the Streets: From Port Huron to the Siege of Chicago*. New York: Simon and Schuster.

Miller, R. 2000. *Researching Life Stories and Family Histories*. London: Sage.

Miller R.L. and Brewer, J.D. (eds) 2003. *A-Z: A Dictionary of Key Social Science Research Concepts*. London: Sage.

Mills, C.W. [1959] 1970. *The Sociological Imagination*. Harmondswoth: Penguin.

Mishra, R. 1999. *Globalisation and the Welfare State*. London: Edward Elgar.

Michelin Guides, 1919. *Ypres and the Battle of Ypres, Illustrated Michelin Guides to the Battlefields*. Clement Ferrand: Michelin and Co., with Easingwold, York: G.H. Smith and Son.

Moody, H.R. 2007. Justice between generations: The recent history of an idea, in *Critical Perspectives on Ageing Societies*, edited by M. Bernard and T. Scharf. Bristol: Policy Press, 125–137.

Morrison, B. 1998. *And When Did You Last See Your Father: A Son's Memoir of Love and Loss*. London: Picador Press.

Murdock, G. and McCron, R. [1976] 1998. Consciousness of class and consciousness of generation, in *Resistance Through Rituals: Youth Subcultures in Post-War Britain*, edited by S. Hall and T. Jefferson. London: Routledge, 192–207.

Mutchler, J.E. 1997. The Sociology of aging: Implications for public policy. *International Journal of Sociology and Social Policy*, 17(9/10), 1–7.

Nash, L. 1978. Concepts of existence: Greek origins of generational thought. *Daedalus*, 107(4), 1–21.

Nesbit, R.A. 1970. *The Social Bond*. New York: Knopf.

Nora, P. 1997. *The Realms of Memory: The Construction of the French Past. Vol I, Conflicts and Divisions*. New York: Columbia Press.

Norris, P., Lovenduski, J. and Campbell, R. 2004. *Closing the Activism Gap: Gender and Political Participation in Britain*. London: The Electoral Commission.

O'Donnell, M. 2001. *Classical and Contemporary Sociology: Theory and Issues*. London: Hodder and Stoughton.

O'Hara, C. 1999. *The Philosophy of Punk: More than Noise!!* AK Distribution.

Offe, C. 1985. *Disorganised Capitalism*. Cambridge: MIT.

Office for National Statistics, 2004. *Focus on Ethnicity and Identity*. London: ONS.

Ortega y Gasset, J. 1928 *The Task of Our Time*, in German, first published (1923) in Spanish from lectures given between 1920–21, no bibliographic record available.

Ortega y Gasset, J. 1933. *The Modern Theme*. New York: W.W. Norton.

Östor, Á. 1993. *Vessels of Time: An Essay on Temporal Change and Social Transformation*. Oxford: Oxford University Press.

Parales, J. 1955. Rebels Without a Cause, and Couldn't Care Less, *New York Times*, July 16, 21.

Patterson, A. and Brown, S. 1999. *The Confessionalist Manifesto: Consumer Behaviour and Self-Construction in High Fidelity and Bridget Jones's Diary*.

University of Ulster, Marketing and Retailing Working Paper Series, No. 99/2.

Patton, M.Q. 2002. *Qualitative Research and Evaluative Methods*. Thousand Oaks, California: Sage.

Penguin. 1998. *Poems of the Great War 1914–1918. Penguin Twentieth Century Classics*. London: Penguin [no author or editor].

Peterson, J. 1930. *Die Literarischen Generationen*. Berlin: Junker and Dunnhaupt.

Peyre, H. 1948. *Les Génèrations Litteraires*. Paris: Bowin.

Pilcher, J. 1994. Mannheim's sociology of generations: An undervalued legacy. *British Journal of Sociology*, 45(3), 481–495.

Pilcher, J. 1995. *Age and Generation in Modern Britain*. Oxford: Oxford University Press.

Pilcher, J. 1998. *Women of their Time: Generation, Gender Issues and Feminism*. Aldershot: Ashgate.

Pilcher, J. 1999. *Women in Contemporary Britain: An Introduction*. London: Routledge.

Pilcher, J. and Wragg, S. 1996. *Thatcher's Children? Politics, Childhood and Society in the 1980s and 1990s*. London: Falmer Press.

Pilcher, J., Pole, C. and Williams, J. 2003. *Editorial Sociological Research Online*, 84.

Preston, S. 1984. Children and the elderly: Divergent paths for America's dependents. *Demography*, 21(4), 435–457.

Proust, M. 1983. *Remembrance of Things Past*. Harmondswoth: Penguin.

Rader, D. 1969. *I Ain't Marchin' Anymore: An Honest Account of Life Amongst the Disaffected Young – their Violence, Politics and Sex*. New York: David McKay.

Radstone, S. (ed.) 2000. *Memory and Methodology*. Oxford: Berg.

Ranelagh, J. 1991. *Thatcher's People*. London: HarperCollins.

Rapport, N. 1997. *Transcendent Individual: Towards a Literary and Liberal Anthropology*. London: Routledge.

Rawls, J. 1971. *A Theory of Justice*. Cambridge: Harvard University Press.

Rayner, D. 1981. *The Payment of Benefits to Unemployed People*. London: HMSO.

Reddish, E. 2003. *The Fourteenth Century Tree of Jesse in the Nave of York Minster in York Medieval Yearbook: MA Essays from the Centre of Medieval Studies*. York: The Centre for Medieval Studies: York University, 2(2), 1–15, available at http://www.york.ac.uk/teaching/history/pjpg/jesse.pdf.

Redford, D.B. 2003. *The Oxford Essential Guide to Egyptian Mythology*. Oxford: Oxford University Press.

Redhead, S. 1990. *The End-of-the-Century Party: Youth and Pop Towards 2000*. Manchester: Manchester University Press.

Remarque, E.M. 1996 [1929]. *All Quiet on the Western Front*. New York: Vintage Classics.

Reynaud, E. 2000. Introduction, in *Pensions in the European Union: Adapting to Economic and Social Change*, edited by G. Hughes and J. Stewart. Boston: Kluwer Academic Publishers.

Ricoeur, P. 1988. *Time and Narrative, Volume 3*. Chicago: University of Chicago Press.

Rivers, W.H. 1918. The repression of war experience. *The Lancet*, 2 February, 173–177.

Ritzer, G. and Goodman, D. 2003. *Sociological Theory*. New York: McGraw Hill.

Roberts, B. 2001. *Biographical Research*. Buckingham: Open University Press.

Roberts, F.J. 1930. *The Wipers Times* London: Everleigh Nash and Grayson Ltd.

Robertson, R. 1992. *Globalisation: Social Theory and Global Culture*. London: Sage.

Rose, R. and Carnaghan, E. 1995. Generational effects on attitudes to communist regimes: A comparative analysis. *Post-Soviet Affairs*, 11(1), 2–56.

Rosch, E. and Lloyd, B.B. 1978. *Cognition and Categorization*. New Jersey: Social Science Research Council Committee on Cognitive Research.

Ruspini, E. and Dale, A. 2002. *The Gender Dimension of Social Change: The Contribution of Dynamic Research to the Study of Women's Life Courses*. Bristol: Policy Press.

Ryder, N. 1965. The cohort as a concept in the study of social change. *American Sociological Review*, 30 (December), 843–861.

Ryder, N. 1985. The cohort as a concept in the study of social change, revision of paper in ASR 30, 843–861, in *Cohort Analysis in Social Research: Beyond the Identification Problem*, edited by W.M. Mason and S.E. Fienberg. New York: Springer-Verlag.

Ryder, N. and Westoff, C. 1977. *The Contraceptive Revolution*. Princeton: Princeton University Press.

SDS 2010 Port Huron Draft Statement, http://www.sds-1960s.org/PortHuron Statement-draft.htm 10/01/10.

SDS 2010 Port Huron Final Statement, http://www.sds-1960s.org/PortHuron Statement-draft.htm 10/01/10.

Sabin, R. 1999. *Punk Rock, So What? The Cultural Legacy of Punk*. London: Routledge.

Sainsbury, D. 1994. *Gendering Welfare States*. London: Sage.

Sakwa, R. and Stevens, A. 2000. *Contemporary Europe*. London: Macmillan.

Samuel, R. 1995. *Theatres of Memory: Past and Present in Contemporary British Culture*. London and New York: Verso.

Sapelli, G. 1995. *Southern Europe Since 1945*. Longman: London.

Sassoon, D. 1997. *Contemporary Italy: Politics, Economy and Society*. Longman: London.

Saunders, P. 1983. *Urban Politics: Sociological Interpretation*. London: Hutchinson.

Schuman, H. and Rieger, C. 1992. Historical analogies, generational effects, and attitudes towards war. *American Sociological Review*, 57, 327–333.

Schuman, H. and Scott, J. 1989. Generations and collective memories. *American Sociological Review*, 54, 359–381.

Schutz, A. 1967. *The Phenomenology of the Social World*. Evanston: Northwestern University Press.

Scott, J. and Zac, L. 1992. *Generations, Collective Memory and Events in Europe*. Paper to British Sociological Association Annual Conference, University of Kent.

Sheehy, G. 1991. *The Silent Passage*. London: HarperCollins.

Sheehy, G. 1996. *New Passages: Making Your Life Across Time*. London: HarperCollins.

Sheffield, G. 2002. *Forgotten Victory: The First World War: Myths and Realities*. London: Headline Review.

Shilling, C. 1993 *The Body and Social Theory*. London: Sage.

Shils, E. 1969. Plenitude and Scarcity. *Encounter*, 32 (May), 37–57.

Siaroff, A. 1994. Work, welfare and gender equality: A new typology, in *Gendering Welfare States*, edited by D. Sainsbury. London: Sage, 82–100.

Smart, C. 2000. *Divorce in England 1950–2000: A Moral Tale?* Working Paper 20, University of Leeds Centre for Research on Family, Kinship and Childhood.

Smith, M. 2009. *Traversing the Afterlife*. Oxford: Oxford University Press.

Stanley, L. 1992. *The Auto/Biographical I; Theory and Practice of Feminist Auto/Biography*. Manchester; Manchester University Press.

Stanworth, M.D. (ed.) 1987. *Reproductive Technologies, Gender, Motherhood and Medicine*. Cambridge: Polity in association with Blackwell.

Stein, J. 2001. Reflections on time, time-space compression and technology in the nineteenth century, in *Timespace: Geographies of Temporality*, edited by J. May and N. Thrift. London: Routledge, 106–119.

Stewart, A.J. and Healy, J.M. 1989. Linking individual development and social change. *American Psychologist*, 44, 30–42.

Strathern, M. 1992. *After Nature: English Kinship in the Late Twentieth Century*. Cambridge: Cambridge University Press.

Strauss, A. and Fagerhaugh, S. 1985. *Social Organisation of Medical Work*. Chicago: University of Chicago Press.

Strauss, W. and Howe, N. 1991. *Generations: The History of America's Future, 1584–2069*. New York: Quill William Morrow.

Sturken, M. 1997. *Tangled Memories: The Vietnam War, the AIDS Epidemic and the Politics of Remembering*. Berkely: University of California Press.

Taylor A.J.P. [1954] 1971. *The Struggle for Mastery in Europe 1948–1918*. Oxford: Oxford University Press.

Terraine, J. 2000 [1963]. *Douglas Haig: The Educated Soldier*. London: Phoenix.

Thane, P. 2000. *Old Age in English History*. Oxford: Clarendon Press.

Thelen, D. 1989. Memory and American History. *Journal of American History*, 75, 117–129.

Thomas, W.I. and Znaniecki, F. [1918–21] 1958. *The Polish Peasant in Europe and America.* New York: Dover Publications.

Thomson, D. 1989. The welfare state and generation conflict: Winners and losers, in *Workers Versus Pensioners: Inter-Generational Justice in an Ageing World,* edited by P. Johnson, C. Conrad and D. Thomson. Manchester: Manchester University Press, 33–56.

Thompson, E.P. 1967. Time, work-discipline, and industrial capitalism. *Past and Present,* 36, 57–97.

Thompson, P. 1978. *The Voice of the Past: Oral History.* Oxford: Oxford University Press.

Thrasher, F. 1927. *The Gang: A Study of 1,313 Gangs in Chicago.* Chicago: University of Chicago Press.

Throsby, K. 2001. *No-One Will Ever Call Me Mummy: Making Sense of the End of IVF Treatment.* London School of Economics, Gender Institute, New Working Paper Series.

Trautmann, T.R. 1987. *Lewis Henry Morgan and the Invention of Kinship.* Berkeley and Los Angeles: University of California Press.

Tuchman, B. 2004 [1962]. *The Guns of August.* New York: First Presidio Press Mass Market Edition.

Turner, B.S. 1998. Ageing and generational conflicts: A reply to Sarah Irwin. *British Journal of Sociology,* 49(2), 299.

Turner, B.S. 2002. Strategic generations: Historical change, literary expression, and generational politics, in *Generational Consciousness, Narrative, and Politics,* edited by J. Edmunds and B.S. Turner. Oxford: Rowman and Littlefield, 13–29.

Turner, V. 1969. *The Ritual Process.* Chicago: Aldine.

Urry, J. 1996. Sociology of time and space, in *The Blackwell Companion to Social Theory,* edited by B.S. Turner. Oxford: Blackwell, 369–428.

Urry, J. and Rojek, C. 1997. *Touring Cultures: Transformations of Travel and Theory.* London: Routledge.

Van den Broek, A. 1995. *Cultural Change: The Impact of Cohort Replacement and the Absence of Generations.* Paper presented at the Second Conference of the European Sociological Association, Budapest, Aug/Sept.

Van Gennep [1908] 1960. *The Rites of Passage.* London: Routledge.

Van Meter, K. 1990. *Methodological and Design Issues: Techniques for Assessing the Representatives of Snowball Sample*s. NIDA Research Monograph, 31–43.

Veblen, T. 1994. *The Theory of the Leisure Class.* London: Penguin.

Vincent, J. 1995. *Inequality and Old Age.* London: UCL.

Vincent, J. 2003. *Old Age.* London: Routledge.

Walby, S. 1990. *Theorizing Patriarchy.* Cambridge: Polity Press.

Walker, A. 1996. *The New Generational Contract.* London: UCL.

Weber, M. [1904] 1930. *The Protestant Work Ethic and the Spirit of Capitalism.* London: George Allen and Unwin.

Weeks, J. 1989. *Sex, Politics and Society: The Regulation of Sexuality since 1800*. London: Longman.

Whithorn, D.P. 2003. *Bringing Uncle Albert Home: A Soldier's Tale*. Stroud, Gloucestershire: Sutton Publishing.

Wilde, L. 1994. *Modern European Socialism*. Aldershot: Dartmouth Publishing Company.

Wilkinson, H. 1994. *No Turning Back: Generations and the Genderquake*. London: Demos.

Williams, A., Coupland, J., Folwell, A. and Sparks, L. 1997. Talking about Generation X: Defining them as they define themselves. *Journal of Language and Social Psychology*, 16(3), 251–277.

Williams, F. 1989. *Social Policy: A Critical Introduction*. Cambridge: Polity Press.

Winch, P. [1958] 1990. *The Idea of a Social Science and its Relation to Philosophy*. London: Routledge.

Winter, J.M. 1995. *Sites of Memory, Sites of Mourning: The Great War in European Cultural History*. Cambridge: Cambridge University Press.

Wipers Times, The. 1916 excerpt, *Ypres Trenches*, 1(4).

Wohl, R. 1980. *The Generation of 1914*. London: Weidenfeld and Nicolson.

Wolff, K.H., Volker, M. and Kettler, D. 1993. *From Karl Mannheim*. New Brunswick, New Jersey: Transaction Publishers.

Wyatt, D. 1993. *Out of the Sixties. Storytelling and the Vietnam Generation*. Cambridge: Cambridge University Press.

Index